ALVIN J. VANDER GRIE

DISCOVER
your
GIFTS

and Learn How to Use Them

STUDENT MANUAL

FAITH
ALIVE®
Christian Resources

Grand Rapids, Michigan

We are grateful to Alvin J. Vander Griend for planning and writing this fully revised edition of *Discover Your Gifts and Learn How to Use Them* (revised and expanded from *Discover Your Gifts*, published by Christian Reformed Home Missions in 1980, revised in 1983).

Unless otherwise indicated, the Scripture quotations in this publication are from the HOLY BIBLE, NEW INTERNATIONAL VERSION, © 1973, 1978, 1984, International Bible Society. Used by permission of Zondervan Bible Publishers.

Scripture quotations accompanied by the abbreviation NCV are from the New Century Version, © 1991 by Word Publishing, Dallas, Texas 75309. Used by permission.

Faith Alive Resources published by CRC Publications.
We welcome your comments. Call us at 1-800-333-8300 or e-mail us at editors@faithaliveresources.org.

ISBN 1-56212-183-9

10 9 8 7 6 5 4 3

CONTENTS

INTRODUCTION

PREFACE

Every Christian is full of potential for service in the kingdom. Potential, however, needs to be developed. Unused, it will waste away.

One day when I needed a flashlight, I went to the glove compartment of my car. I found a flashlight all right, but it didn't work. I wasn't surprised. It hadn't been used in years. When I unscrewed the cap to check the batteries, I found an even worse problem. The batteries had burst, and corrosive acid had leaked all over the inside of the flashlight. Designed to produce light, the unused batteries had instead destroyed the very possibility of light.

It's that way with spiritual gifts too. Meant to be assets in the kingdom, they may actually become liabilities if not discovered, developed, and used. *Discover Your Gifts and Learn How to Use Them* is intended to prevent that from happening in your church. It's a Bible course about special abilities called spiritual gifts, which God in his grace has given to each believer. In this course you will learn what spiritual gifts are, why God has given them, how they are to be used, and how they can be abused. And along the way you'll learn about the spiritual gifts *you've* been given, including potential gifts that God is working in you to develop.

There are three parts to this manual:

Part A: Gift Sessions contains seven study sessions on spiritual gifts. Each session includes a Bible-discovery section, a section reviewing three spiritual gifts, an interaction section, and a personal-application section. Supplementary reading material is found at the end of each session.

Part B: Assessment Forms includes the Spiritual Gift Discovery Questionnaire and other forms that assess the participant's temperament, ministry passion, skills/talents, spiritual maturity, and availability. These are used with sessions 3 and 5 of the course.

Part C: Gift Studies contains studies of twenty-one individual spiritual gifts. Each study includes the following sections: definition of the gift, scriptural explanation, characteristics of the user, uses of the gift, potential liabilities, responsibility of all Christians, discerning the gift, and an exploring exercise in Scripture. These gift studies are designed to be read and studied by participants at home after each class session.

God intends each believer to be a channel of God's grace to others. Using our spiritual gifts is one of the primary ways we fulfill this function in God's kingdom. *Discover Your Gifts and Learn How to Use Them* is a proven tool to help you know your "spiritual job description" and be God's instrument of grace in this needy world. It's a pathway of joy.

You are starting on an exciting and challenging journey. Pray that God will give you the courage and the perseverance to complete it. You will likely experience opposition from the evil one. The devil wants to render Christians ineffective, and he often works in very subtle ways. But Christ has come to destroy the work of the devil (1 John 3:8), and by his Spirit he equips us with gifts to minister in ways that seriously threaten the devil's cause. God wants you to be effective and fruitful for him, and he is most eager to support and strengthen you as you work with other believers to build up the one body of Christ and glorify him (1 Corinthians 12). The prayer "help me to know and use my gifts for you" is a prayer that rings true with God's will, and he will be quick to answer.

GUIDELINES

The following guidelines will help you make the best use of this material.

1. **Take the challenge of the course seriously.** The primary challenge is not simply to learn about spiritual gifts. It is to discover *your* gifts and to put them to use in the kingdom of God. God desires and expects our best. That means giving our best in this course and our best in using our grace-given gifts for him.

2. **Participate vigorously in the small groups.** Every class session will provide opportunity to work in small groups. This will give everyone an opportunity to give input and ask questions. Jump into small group times with a bit of "reckless abandon." Share yourself and your thoughts as freely and fully as possible. Openly accept others and their contributions. In a learning context all questions and comments are valuable.

3. **Read carefully the pages "For Added Insight" at the end of each session.** The questions you will find in these pages are most often asked today. Reading and studying these pages each week will reinforce and extend what you have learned in the class session.

4. **Take time to learn about each individual gift as assigned.** You'll grow to understand God's plan, the Christian community, your spiritually gifted friends, and yourself better if you know something about each of the spiritual gifts God has given. Give extra effort to learning about the gifts you have identified as your own.

5. **When the course is finished, work with a placement consultant until you've found the ministry that's right for you.** Schedule time with a placement consultant **immediately** after finishing the course. This will be a time to review the results of the assessment forms (found in Part B of this manual) and to determine, with the consultant's help, which ministry tasks you are best fitted for and to learn which tasks are available in your church or community. **This step should not be omitted.** Without it the value of the course will be negligible.

6. **Get into ministry.** Get started in a gift-related ministry as soon as possible, but don't bite off too much at the outset. Be willing to start small. It may be best to work as an apprentice with someone else first. Learn initially by watching, next by working under supervision, and then finally by working without supervision. *Note:* No one's work in ministry should ever be attempted completely alone or in one's own strength. We are all accountable to each other in the body of Christ—and ultimately to our Lord and Master. Pray continually that you not be tempted to act on your own, without the leading of the Holy Spirit. Test your impulses by asking for the Spirit's guidance, for whoever asks sincerely in Jesus' name will not be refused (John 14:12-14; James 1:5).

7. **Get support.** There should be no ministry without support. Start by securing the prayer support of other interested individuals. Look for others in similar ministries with whom you can meet in order to share ideas, talk about issues, brainstorm, and ask questions. It will take some extra time, but, in the long run, your ministry in Christ will benefit greatly from the support of other believers.

GIFT SESSIONS

Part A

CHRIST AND HIS GIFTS

Opening Prayer

Preview

In this session we will

- discover seven basic spiritual-gift concepts from Scripture.

- develop a definition of spiritual gifts.

- explore the spiritual gifts of administration, leadership, and creative ability.

Step 1: Warm-up Exercise

In small groups of three introduce yourselves to each other and tell about one special gift (of any kind) that you remember receiving.

Step 2: Bible Discovery

Basic Bible Concepts

Take a look at the following Bible passages on spiritual gifts. Each group of passages conveys a basic spiritual-gift concept. Working in your small groups, read the passages and write down *the main idea* found in each set of verses. This will be an idea that flows through all the verses.

Ephesians 4:11 (NCV) Christ gave gifts to people.

1 Corinthians 12:8 To one there is given through the Spirit . . .

1 Corinthians 12:11 (NCV) One Spirit, the same Spirit, does all these things, and the Spirit decides what to give each person.

Main Idea 1:

1 Corinthians 12:7 To each one the manifestation of the Spirit is given.

1 Peter 4:10 Each one should use whatever gift . . .

Main Idea 2:

Romans 12:6 We have . . . gifts, according to the grace given us.

Ephesians 4:7 To each one of us grace has been given as Christ apportioned it.

1 Peter 4:10 Serve others, faithfully administering God's grace in its various forms.

Main Idea 3:

Romans 12:6 We have different gifts. . . .

1 Corinthians 12:8-10 ⁸To one there is given through the Spirit the message of wisdom, to another the message of knowledge . . . ⁹to another faith . . . to another gifts of healing . . . ¹⁰to another miraculous powers, to another . . . to another . . . to another . . .

1 Corinthians 12:28 In the church God has appointed first of all apostles, second prophets, third teachers, then workers of miracles, also those having gifts of healing, those able to help others, those with gifts of administration, and those speaking in different kinds of tongues.

Main Idea 4:

1 Corinthians 12:7 To each one . . . [gifts are] given for the common good.

Ephesians 4:8, 12 [8][Christ] gave gifts . . . [12]to prepare God's people for works of service, so that the body of Christ may be built up.

1 Peter 4:10 Each one should use whatever gift . . . to serve others.

Main Idea 5:

1 Corinthians 12:13-14 We were all baptized by one Spirit into one body. . . . Now the body is not made up of one part but of many.

1 Corinthians 12:27 You are the body of Christ, and each one of you is a part of it.

Romans 12:5 In Christ we who are many form one body, and each member belongs to all the others.

Main Idea 6:

1 Corinthians 13:1-3 (NCV) [1]I may speak in different languages. . . . But if I do not have love, I am only a noisy bell or a crashing cymbal. [2]I may have the gift of prophecy. I may understand all the secret things of God and have all knowledge, and I may have faith so great I can move mountains. But even with all these things, if I do not have love, then I am nothing. [3]I may give away everything I have, and I may even give my body as an offering to be burned. But I gain nothing if I do not have love.

Main Idea 7:

Step 3: Defining Spiritual Gifts

Spiritual gifts are special abilities given by Christ through the Holy Spirit to empower believers for the ministries of the body.

- special abilities—

- given by Christ—

- through the Holy Spirit—

- to empower believers—

- for the ministries of the body—

Step 4: Exploring Individual Gifts

1. **Administration**—The special Spirit-given ability to design and execute a plan of action through which a number of believers are enabled to work effectively together to do the Lord's work.

   1 Corinthians 12:28 In the church God has appointed . . . those with gifts of administration.

   a. **The basic idea**—

   b. **Distinguished from leadership**—

   c. **Administration as a role**—

2. **Leadership**—The special Spirit-given ability to lead others by seeing and casting a vision, setting and communicating goals, and inspiring and directing people to work together toward those goals.

   Romans 12:8 (NCV) Anyone who has the gift of being a leader should try hard when he leads.

   a. **The basic idea**—

   b. **A biblical model**—

   c. **Leadership as a role**—

3. **Creative Ability**—The special Spirit-given ability to communicate truth and advance God's kingdom through creative means such as music, drama, visual arts, graphic arts, and writing skills.

   Exodus 35:31 He has filled [them] with the Spirit of God, with skill, ability and knowledge in all kinds of crafts.

   a. **The basic idea**—

   b. **A multiple gift**—

   c. **Creative ability as a role**—

Step 5: Interaction

As time permits, discuss the following questions:

1. How would you respond to a Christian who said, "I can't do anything well. I don't have any spiritual gifts"?

2. In the light of what Scripture says about gifts, how would you counsel a Christian who is dissatisfied with his or her gifts and is envious of the gifts of others?

Personal Application

Give thanks to God for the gifts he has given you (even if you don't know what they are yet) and for the privilege of being a ministering member of his body. Ask for the Holy Spirit's wisdom and insight in understanding what spiritual gifts are and why he has given them to the church.

After the Session

Read For Added Insight (next page) after this session is finished. Also read about the gifts of administration, leadership, and creative ability in Part C—Gift Studies of this manual. Doing the brief Bible study at the end of each gift study will deepen your understanding of the gift discussed there. This exercise will be especially valuable if you have the gift you are studying.

FOR ADDED INSIGHT

Why study spiritual gifts?

There are several good reasons to study spiritual gifts. First, it's a matter of obedience. The apostle Paul warns "Now about spiritual gifts . . . I do not want you to be ignorant" (1 Corinthians 12:1). Second, the church will benefit and its ministries will become increasingly effective as its members discover and use their gifts. Third, individual believers will mature in their self-image and faith as they sense the competence God has given them.

What are spiritual gifts?

Spiritual gifts are special abilities given by Christ through the Holy Spirit to empower believers for the ministries of the body. It's helpful to look at each phrase of this definition separately.

- **special abilities**—These are abilities that exceed the normal ability level of others in the church to do something well for the Lord. Special abilities are valuable because the possessor is able to make a distinctive contribution with the gift. Each special ability is important to the well-being of the whole. New believers often find that these special abilities are similar to or complement natural talents they possessed before they came to faith. Sometimes, however, these abilities are radically new and different from pre-Christian abilities.

- **given by Christ**—Christ, from his throne in heaven, continues to be active in this world, exercising his lordship in and through believers by providing them with unique powers for ministry. With these powers believers accomplish his tasks on earth and exercise his authority over the powers of darkness.

- **through the Holy Spirit**—The Holy Spirit, working with the Father and the Son (see 1 Corinthians 12:4-11), provides the motivation, energy, and guidance to undergird the gifted person. The Spirit is able to operate this way from his place within the heart of the believer. He moves in response to our asking and faithful obedience.

- **to empower believers**—Power from the Holy Spirit translates into ability or competence that causes the gifted person to act. This power is given as a continuing operation within, not something delivered once and for all to a believer. Every believer has one or more spiritual gifts. Unbelievers do not receive spiritual gifts. They, of course, have abilities which come from God, but these abilities do not warrant the name spiritual gifts since they are not used under the direction of the Holy Spirit or for advancing the kingdom of God.

- **for the ministries of the body**—Gifts are given so that believers may engage in acts of service that build up the church, Christ's body, and advance his kingdom in the world.

Why are spiritual gifts given?

The Holy Spirit gives spiritual gifts for three reasons:

- **that Christians may minister to each other in the body of Christ.** The apostle Paul states that gifts are given "for the common good" (1 Corinthians 12:7). The apostle Peter says we ought to use our gifts "to serve others" (1 Peter 4:10).

- **"that the body of Christ may be built up"—that is, grow in unity and maturity in Christ (Ephesians 4:11-16).** As believers use their gifts, the church's witness and ministry are extended in the world.

- **that God may be glorified.** Peter observes that God will be glorified in everything if believers, exercising their gifts, speak the words of God and serve in the strength which God supplies (1 Peter 4:11).

Individual believers experience satisfaction by knowing that their gifts are useful in service to the Master. Believers' sense of belonging to Christ and his church is also strengthened as they use their gifts.

Why the renewed interest in spiritual gifts today?

This interest has been kindled by several factors:

- **The impact of charismatic renewal.** The charismatic movement, though sometimes extreme, has brought about a new interest in the work of the Holy Spirit. Partly because of charismatics' excesses and partly because of their vitality, mainline churches have taken a new look at spiritual gifts.

- **A renewed concern for the ministry of all believers.** Within the past few decades increasing interest in the ministry of all believers has caused the church to re-examine the biblical role of its members. The ministry role of believers is rooted in spiritual gifts, the means by which they are empowered for service. The clergy's tendency to usurp the ministry roles that God intended for the members is being called into question.

- **The search for intimate, less institutionalized structures.** Many church leaders today are discontented with the structures of the past. They desire to find new and better forms for Christian communal life. Their quest has led them back to the Scriptures for a fresh look at life in the New Testament church. They have concluded that structures based on top-down authority need to be replaced by structures that acknowledge the spiritual giftedness of members.

Am I already using all the gifts I will ever have?

It's important also to know that while we have spiritual gifts that we are using right now, we often have the potential for developing various other gifts. As we grow more and more mature in Christ, God molds us and gifts us to serve in various ways—sometimes in ways we would not have pursued or even imagined without the guiding of the Holy Spirit.

A spiritual gift you are using right now is called a *working gift.* You may not even be aware you have a certain working gift, but it's one you are using nonetheless. A spiritual gift that you may have the potential for developing, on the other hand, is called a *waiting gift.* You can usually identify a waiting gift by examining your interests, inclinations, sensitivities, and concerns. You'll be able to discover which working gifts and waiting gifts you have when you complete the Spiritual Gift Discovery Questionnaire after session 3.

Session 2

NAMING THE GIFTS

Opening Prayer

Preview

In this session we will

- examine New Testament passages that name spiritual gifts.

- learn how the New Testament categorizes gifts.

- explore the spiritual gifts of shepherding, teaching, and evangelism.

Step 1: Bible Discovery

Identifying Spiritual Gifts

Below are four of the main Bible passages on spiritual gifts. Working alone, read each passage, identify the gifts named in that passage, and list them in the blanks that follow. When you have listed all the gifts, cross out duplicates and count the remaining number of gifts. Be sure to count each gift only once.

Romans 12:6-8 (NCV) [6]We all have different gifts, each of which came because of the grace God gave us. The person who has the gift of prophecy should use that gift in agreement with the faith. [7]Anyone who has the gift of serving should serve. Anyone who has the gift of teaching should teach. [8]Whoever has the gift of encouraging others should encourage. Whoever has the gift of giving to others should give freely. Anyone who has the gift of being a leader should try hard when he leads. Whoever has the gift of showing mercy to others should do so with joy.

1. _____
2. _____
3. _____
4. _____
5. _____
6. _____
7. _____

1 Corinthians 12:7-11 (NCV) [7]Something from the Spirit can be seen in each person, for the common good. [8]The Spirit gives one person the ability to speak with wisdom, and the same Spirit gives another the ability to speak with knowledge. [9]The same Spirit gives faith to one person.

And, to another, that one Spirit gives gifts of healing. [10]The Spirit gives to another person the power to do miracles, to another the ability to prophesy. And he gives to another the ability to know the difference between good and evil spirits. The Spirit gives one person the ability to speak in different kinds of languages and to another the ability to interpret those languages. [11]One Spirit, the same Spirit, does all these things, and the Spirit decides what to give each person.

1. _____
2. _____
3. _____
4. _____
5. _____
6. _____
7. _____
8. _____
9. _____

1 Corinthians 12:27-31 [27]Now you are the body of Christ, and each one of you is a part of it. [28]And in the church God has appointed first of all apostles, second prophets, third teachers, then workers of miracles, also those having gifts of healing, those able to help others, those with gifts of administration, and those speaking in different kinds of tongues. [29]Are all apostles? Are all prophets? Are all teachers? Do all work miracles? [30]Do all have gifts of healing? Do all speak in tongues? Do all interpret? [31]But eagerly desire the greater gifts.

1. _____
2. _____
3. _____
4. _____
5. _____
6. _____
7. _____
8. _____
9. _____

Ephesians 4:8, 11-12 ⁸"When [Christ] ascended on high, he led captives in his train and gave gifts to [people]. . . ." ¹¹It was he who gave some to be apostles, some to be prophets, some to be evangelists, and some to be pastors and teachers, ¹²to prepare God's people for works of service, so that the body of Christ may be built up. . . .

1. _____
2. _____
3. _____
4. _____
5. _____

Cross out any duplicates in your lists. How many gifts are left? _____

Different Types of Gifts

Read this passage and answer the following questions.

1 Peter 4:10-11 (NCV) ¹⁰Each of you has received a gift to use to serve others. Be good servants of God's various gifts of grace. ¹¹Anyone who speaks should speak words from God. Anyone who serves should serve with the strength God gives so that in everything God will be praised through Jesus Christ.

1. What type of gifts does verse 11a mention?

2. Describe in your own words how this type of gift is to be used.

3. Which of the gifts listed in Step 1 above are probably "speaking gifts"?

4. What type of gifts does verse 11b mention?

5. Describe how this type of gift is to be used.

6. Which of the gifts listed in Step 1 above are probably "serving gifts"?

Step 2: Interaction

1. Use the following questions to review together the work completed in Step 1.

   a. How many gifts are listed in the passages studied in Step 1?

   b. What are the two types of gifts in 1 Peter 4:10-11?

   c. According to 1 Peter 4:10-11, what is God's role with regard to gifts? What is the gifted person's role?

2. Discuss these additional questions together:

a. Are there spiritual gifts in use today that are not mentioned in the New Testament?

b. Are some gifts that are mentioned in the Bible no longer valid?

c. Are all spiritual gifts equal?

3. When your leader has read aloud this quote by A. T. Pierson, discuss it in small groups of three by answering the questions below.

Everyone has some gift, therefore all should be encouraged. No one has all gifts, therefore all should be humble. All gifts are for the one Body, therefore all should be harmonious. All gifts are from the Lord, therefore all should be contented. All gifts are mutually helpful and needful, therefore all should be studiously faithful. All gifts promote the health and strength of the whole Body, therefore none can easily be dispensed with. All gifts depend on his fullness for power, therefore all should keep in close touch with him.

—from *The Holy Spirit and His Gifts* by J. Oswald Sanders (Zondervan, 1970)

a. How can awareness of gifts bring personal encouragement, humility, and contentment?

b. What are some specific ways in which gifts "promote the health and strength of the whole Body"? In what ways have you personally been blessed when others have used their gifts for you?

c. How important is it for *all* the gifts to be used in the church?

Step 3: Exploring Individual Gifts

1. **Shepherding**—The special Spirit-given ability to keep watch over, care for, and feed members of the body of Christ, guiding, admonishing, and discipling them toward spiritual maturity.

Ephesians 4:11 He . . . gave some to be . . . pastors [shepherds].

a. **The basic idea—**

b. **Not an office—**

c. **Shepherding as a role—**

2. **Teaching**—The special Spirit-given ability to clearly and effectively communicate biblical truths and information that helps believers mature in the faith, building up the body of Christ.

Romans 12:7 (NCV) Anyone who has the gift of teaching should teach. (See also Ephesians 4:11-12.)

a. **The basic idea—**

b. **Modeled by Jesus and his disciples—**

c. **Teaching as a role—**

3. **Evangelism**—The special Spirit-given ability to present the gospel to unbelievers in clear and meaningful ways that bring a positive response.

Ephesians 4:11 He . . . gave some to be . . . evangelists.

a. **The basic idea—**

b. **Gifted evangelists as equippers—**

c. **Evangelism as a role—**

Personal Application

Thank God for making the church a multigifted body that is able, by the Spirit's power, to advance the kingdom of God in this world. Ask the Holy Spirit to help you know where and how you fit into the body of Christ and how your giftedness is important to the cause of God's kingdom.

After the Session

Read the section For Added Insight, which follows. Also read about the gifts of shepherding, teaching, and evangelism in the Gift Studies section of this manual. Doing the brief Bible study at the end of each gift study will deepen your understanding of the gift. This exercise will be especially valuable if you have the gift you are studying.

FOR ADDED INSIGHT

By now you have named a number of gifts found in four New Testament passages. Remember that some of these gifts actually do belong to you. Before you finish this course, you'll want to be sure that you are able to name your own gifts. Imagine yourself saying to a friend, "I have the spiritual gifts of _____ and _____." That's the most important kind of naming you can do. And it's not arrogant to speak in this way about something God has given you. It honors God, as long as you emphasize that the credit goes to him.

Can a person have more than one spiritual gift?

Most Christians have more than one spiritual gift. New Testament Christians surely did. Philip, for instance, apparently had at least four gifts: wisdom, service, mercy, and evangelism. The apostle Paul obviously had the gifts of teaching and leadership. In addition, he specifically refers to his gifts of prophecy and tongue-speaking (1 Corinthians 14:18, 37). Other apostles were also gifted in several ways. (See Acts 6 and 8.)

A combination of spiritual gifts given to a Christian is called a gift mix. A person's gift mix will usually determine a ministry direction. A person with the gifts of mercy, leadership, and administration, for example, will make a good director of a convalescent home. A person whose gift mix is hospitality, mercy, and encouragement will likely do well in assisting a displaced family in resettlement. A person who has gifts of evangelism and teaching should do a good job leading an evangelistic Bible study group.

How many spiritual gifts are there?

The Bible does not establish a definite number of spiritual gifts. In the first place, the words Paul uses to identify gifts do not always identify clear categories. It is difficult to know, for example, whether a gift such as "utterance of knowledge" is the same as or different from "teaching." "Service" and "helping others" may be identical, or they may be two different but closely related gifts. We simply don't know for sure. Various Scripture passages list various gifts, but there is nothing to suggest that the sum total of these provides a complete and final list.

It is probably best to regard every Spirit-given, Spirit-directed, and Spirit-empowered ability that is used for building up the body of Christ as a spiritual gift, regardless of what one might name it.

Are there spiritual gifts not mentioned in the New Testament?

Many significant abilities being used in ministries today are not specifically mentioned in the New Testament as spiritual gifts. Those who are involved in defending the faith; leading in worship; fund-raising; providing Christian medical, psychological, and social care; tutoring mentally impaired persons; foster parenting; performing or directing in the fine arts, such as music, dance, drama, storytelling, and public speaking; and so on are probably exercising spiritual gifts if they're using them in the Lord's service. Some of these may just be contemporary names for spiritual gifts that are actually listed in the New Testament. Others may be ministries that are possible because of a particular gift mix. Still others may be actual gifts that differ from anything mentioned in the Bible's passages on gifts. The array of gifts in the New Testament reflects life in the early church. Since that time the Holy Spirit has continued to empower believers for service in a rich variety of ways.

Are some gifts mentioned in the Bible no longer valid?

According to some biblical scholars, certain spiritual gifts were necessary to lay the foundations of the early church. Since that has been accomplished, they believe, those gifts are no longer operative. Gifts such as apostleship, prophecy, tongues, healing, and miracles are thought to be in this category.

Other scholars find no warrant from the Scriptures to declare that any gift has ceased. They argue that the Holy Spirit is free to use whatever gifts may suit his purposes in any age. This being true, they believe that believers today should welcome any and all gifts that are given. In *Community of the King,* Howard A. Snyder writes, "The question is whether the Spirit still gives gifts to men, and the answer is yes. Precisely which gifts He gives in any particular age is God's prerogative, and we should not prejudge God."

To Snyder the question of whether certain spiritual gifts are valid is less important than the awakening of gifts within the church. In *The Problem of Wineskins,* he writes, "The function of the local church should be to expect, identify, and awaken the varied gifts that sleep within the community of believers. We can be sure . . . that God will give to each local church all the gifts really necessary for its own upbuilding in love."

Let the church begin by discovering, developing, and using gifts that are currently acknowledged and needed for ministries. Let us further recognize the freedom of the Spirit to bestow his gifts according to his will, and let us be open to the full spectrum of the gifts and provide for the free exercise of all genuine gifts of the Spirit.

Are all gifts equal?

The Bible does not classify specific gifts as "greater" or "lesser." It points to the rich variety of gifts that the Spirit supplies in his work among his people. Every gift is important in the church of Christ. All gifts are interrelated, and none functions well in isolation from other gifts. That each member has been given a different gift or gift mix calls for rejoicing.

Spiritual gifts fall into two categories or types which together enable Christians to do their work in the church and in the world. The first type is *speaking gifts* (prophecy, teaching, encouragement), and the other is *serving gifts* (giving, service, mercy, craftsmanship). The speaking gifts help the church to communicate God's Word; the serving gifts provide the means for doing hands-on ministry.

The words of 1 Corinthians 12:31, "But eagerly desire the greater gifts," suggest that some gifts are more important than others. However, both the verb and the object in this sentence are plural. So the mandate is directed not to individual Christians but to the church in general. The church communally, not individually, should desire the gifts that will help build it, not those that will make the most show.

Do we keep the same spiritual gifts all our lives?

The New Testament gives us no reason to believe that gifts are temporary possessions. Gifts are an integral part of who we are. Ordinarily they are lifetime trusts. It is possible, however, for gifts to become dormant if they are not developed and used. Paul reminds Timothy, "Do not neglect your gift" (1 Timothy 4:14), and later he challenges Timothy to "Fan into flame the gift of God, which is in you" (2 Timothy 1:6). As we move from one situation to another in our lives, a gift may be temporarily shelved if opportunities to use it are not readily available. This doesn't mean, however, that the gift is lost.

It may also happen that as the Lord leads a person into new situations, he also awakens gifts of which the person was previously unaware. For example, this can happen to a parent in middle age whose decreasing childcare responsibilities open up new opportunities for service; it can also happen to an active person who has been paralyzed in an accident. We should be open at all times to the Holy Spirit's call to new ministries that require a different gift mix.

DISCOVERING MY GIFTS

Opening Prayer

Preview

In this session we will

- learn the benefits of discovering and using spiritual gifts.
- learn how to discover spiritual gifts.
- explore the spiritual gifts of mercy, service, and encouragement.

Step 1: The Benefits of Knowing My Spiritual Gifts

1. Divide into groups of three. Discuss the question "How might knowing my spiritual gifts help me?"

2. Five ways we can benefit from knowing our spiritual gifts:

   a.

   b.

   c.

   d.

   e.

Step 2: How to Discover My Spiritual Gifts

The following eight points outline how you can discover your gifts for ministry in the Lord's service.

1. **Understand the gifts.**

2. **Accept that you are gifted.** The Bible says you are, so that settles it.

   a. Read the following Scripture verse, 1 Corinthians 12:7, and write your name in the blank: "Now to _____ the manifestation of the Spirit is given for the common good." A list of the gifts given by the Spirit follows in verses 8-11.

   b. Some of your gifts may be *working gifts;* others may be *waiting gifts.*

3. **Dedicate yourself to ministry.** Tell God you are willing to use your gifts in any way he wants you to.

4. **Pray for guidance.** God will give wisdom and understanding to those who desire it (James 1:5).

   Exercise: Spend time in personal prayer dedicating yourself to the Lord's service and seeking his guidance.

5. **Analyze yourself.** Assume that God is already at work in you and through you. Try to discover your gifts by looking at what God is doing in your life. Take a few minutes to ask yourself the following questions:

   a. What are my interests?

   b. What have I done well in the past?

   c. What do I really get excited about?

   d. What needs am I most aware of in my church and/or community?

   Note: Between this session and the next you will complete the Spiritual Gift Discovery Questionnaire. It will enable you to identify the gifts you may have.

6. **Seek confirmation from other Christians.**

   Exercise: Gather into groups of six. Report briefly to each other your answers to the questions in point 5 above. Be prepared to offer additional input and affirming comments after each person's report.

7. **Get involved in ministry.** You will never know your abilities until you begin to act.

8. **Evaluate the results.** If you are using your gifts in ministry, you should soon begin to see confirming results.

Step 3: Exploring Individual Gifts

1. **Mercy**—The special Spirit-given ability to feel genuine empathy and compassion for hurting people and to translate that feeling into cheerful acts of service.

   Romans 12:8 (NCV) Whoever has the gift of showing mercy to others should do so with joy.

   a. **The basic idea—**

   b. **Demonstrated by action—**

   c. **Mercy as a role—**

2. **Service**—The special Spirit-given ability to see and meet the needs of others by willingly helping them in practical ways.

   Romans 12:7 (NCV) Anyone who has the gift of serving should serve.

   a. **The basic idea—**

   b. **Modeled by many in the New Testament—**

   c. **Service as a role—**

3. **Encouragement**—The special Spirit-given ability to effectively encourage, comfort, challenge, or rebuke others to help them live lives worthy of God.

   Romans 12:8 (NCV) Whoever has the gift of encouraging others should encourage.

   a. **The basic idea—**

   b. **A ministry similar to that of the Holy Spirit—**

   c. **Encouragement as a role—**

Personal Application

Praise God for the power of his Holy Spirit given to members of the body for ministry. Thank God specifically for the gifts he has given you. Ask for wisdom and guidance through the Holy Spirit to understand and develop your particular gifts and to find a place where they may be used in building up the church. Commit yourself before the Lord to use these gifts for his glory.

After the Session

Complete the Spiritual Gift Discovery Questionnaire, located at the beginning of Part B in this manual. Work through the Key Chart (which follows the questionnaire) to list your probable working and waiting gifts.

Read the section For Added Insight, which follows this session. Also do the gift studies on mercy, service, and encouragement in Part C of this manual. Studying especially the spiritual gifts you may have will serve as a foundation for the growth and development of those gifts.

FOR ADDED INSIGHT

For centuries the church seemed blind to the power of spiritual gifts. However, in the past two decades that situation has changed dramatically. This does not mean that the church was devoid of gift ministry for all those years. Many church members were using spiritual gifts long before the advent of gift-discovery programs. It's not necessary to know gifts in order to use them. The church wouldn't have taken the gospel to the nations and brought multitudes into the kingdom if its members had not used their gifts in ministry.

But there's much to be gained by being intentional about gift discovery. Discovering our spiritual gifts brings with it a clearer sense of God's will for our lives. It also provides a whole new perspective on the church and an awareness of the important role of each member. It helps us see the church as a dynamic living organism, a ministering body with living members. It contributes greatly to the mobilization of the *whole* church.

What hinders Christians from discovering their spiritual gifts?

A number of things may hinder a Christian from discovering his or her spiritual gifts:

- **Lack of ministry experience.** Christians often discover that they have a spiritual gift when they experience success in a particular ministry. Those not involved in ministry will not have this opportunity for gift discovery. For this reason new converts, who have little or no experience in ministering, may have more difficulty discovering their gifts. New converts and those with little ministry experience are able, however, to discover gifts that they have a potential for developing. In this course we call those gifts *waiting gifts,* and a person discovers them by carefully monitoring his or her abilities, desires, interests, and inclinations.

- **Disobedience.** Obedience leads to discovery of gifts; disobedience, or not taking one's place of service in the church, may hinder discovery. A Christian who is not being merciful will not likely discover a gift of mercy in himself or herself. A Christian who is not committed to giving faithfully is not likely to develop the gift of giving.

- **Lack of commitment.** Believers who are not committed to using their gifts sacrificially should not expect God's help in uncovering their gifts. Gifts are not for *knowing;* they are for *using.* Commitment to using our gifts is the first step toward discovering them.

- **An unloving spirit.** Gift ministries must always be ministries of love. According to the apostle Paul, gifts and ministries without love are worth nothing (1 Corinthians 13:1-3). If we seek to discover gifts without the motive of love, even our seeking will be hindered.

- **Lack of prayer.** James chided early Christians whose desires were not fulfilled: "You do not have, because you do not ask God" (James 4:2). God wants us to ask for "good gifts" (Luke 11:13), and God is committed to answering when we ask "according to his will" (1 John 5:14). Gifts are among the good things God gives, and it is his will for us to know them. If we ask in faith for knowledge of our gifts, he will not disappoint us.

What role does the family play in gift discovery and use?

The family is the basic unit of the church. The family's involvement in spiritual gifts is important.

First, parents are responsible to teach their children about spiritual things. In Deuteronomy 6:7 the Lord tells parents, "Impress [my commands] on your children. Talk about them when you sit at home and when you walk along the road, when you lie down and when you get up." Parents are first in line when it comes to teaching children about gifts and ministries.

Second, parents are in the best position to observe each child's unique and developing abilities and to affirm each child as a gifted member of the body of Christ. God shapes the lives of his children for ministry from their earliest years onward. Alert parents can see spiritual gifts in bud form.

Third, Christian parents have an ongoing opportunity to set good examples for their children. Their modeling is particularly important in those areas that will become a child's gift areas. For example, parents sharing their faith with others may lay important foundations for a child to whom God gives the gift of evangelism. Parents who give generously and regularly are models who establish patterns for their children who may receive the gift of giving.

Finally, love must motivate the use of all gifts. Parents who, by their example, create a loving atmosphere in their home prepare their children for love-motivated ministries in the future.

GUARDING THE GIFTS

Opening Prayer

Preview

In this session we will

- study the abuse of spiritual gifts discussed in 1 Corinthians 12-14.

- consider misuse of spiritual gifts today.

- explore the spiritual gifts of wisdom, knowledge, and discernment.

Step 1: Warm-up Exercise

As a group, use the following questions to share your experience with the Spiritual Gift Discovery Questionnaire.

1. Were you surprised by the results of the questionnaire?

2. Do you think you should tell others what gifts you have? What are the dangers in this? What are the benefits?

3. What questions do you have about the questionnaire or the results?

Step 2: Bible Discovery

1. Pair off and read the following Bible passages. Describe the problems the Corinthians were having with spiritual gifts. In most cases the problem will need to be deduced from the correction that is proposed in the text.

   1 Corinthians 12:1 Now about spiritual gifts, brothers [and sisters], I do not want you to be ignorant.

   Problem:

   1 Corinthians 12:14-16, 21 [14]Now the body is not made up of one part but of many. [15]If the foot should say, "Because I am not a hand, I do not belong to the body," it would not for that reason cease to be part of the body. [16]And if the ear should say, "Because I am not an eye, I do not belong to the body," it would not for that reason cease to be part of the body. . . . [21]The eye cannot say to the hand, "I don't need you!" And the head cannot say to the feet, "I don't need you!"

   Problem:

   1 Corinthians 12:27-30 [27]Now you are the body of Christ, and each one of you is a part of it. [28]And in the church God has appointed first of all apostles, second prophets, third teachers, then workers of miracles, also those having gifts of healing, those able to help others, those with gifts of administration, and those speaking in different kinds of tongues. [29]Are all apostles? Are all prophets? Are all teachers? Do all work miracles? [30]Do all have gifts of healing? Do all speak in tongues? Do all interpret?

   Problem:

   1 Corinthians 13:1-3 (NCV) [1]I may speak in different languages of people or even angels. But if I do not have love, I am only a noisy bell or a crashing cymbal. [2]I may have the gift of prophecy. I may understand all the secret things of God and have all knowledge, and I may have faith so great I can move mountains. But even with all these things, if I do not have love, then I am nothing. [3]I may give away everything I have, and I may even give my body as an offering to be burned. But I gain nothing if I do not have love.

   Problem:

1 Corinthians 14:1-5 (NCV) [1]You should seek after love, and you should truly want to have the spiritual gifts, especially the gift of prophecy. [2]I will explain why. Those who have the gift of speaking in different languages are not speaking to people; they are speaking to God. No one understands them; they are speaking secret things through the Spirit. [3]But those who prophesy are speaking to people to give them strength, encouragement, and comfort. [4]The ones who speak in different languages are helping only themselves, but those who prophesy are helping the whole church. [5]I wish all of you had the gift of speaking in different kinds of languages, but more, I wish you would prophesy. Those who prophesy are greater than those who can only speak in different languages—unless someone is there who can explain what is said so that the whole church can be helped.

Problem:

1 Corinthians 14:26-28, 40 [26]What then shall we say, brothers [and sisters]? When you come together, everyone has a hymn, or a word of instruction, a revelation, a tongue or an interpretation. All of these must be done for the strengthening of the church. [27]If anyone speaks in a tongue, two—or at the most three—should speak, one at a time, and someone must interpret. [28]If there is no interpreter, the speaker should keep quiet in the church and speak to himself and God. . . . [40]Everything should be done in a fitting and orderly way.

Problem:

2. Gather together as one large group again and review the problems you discerned in the above Scripture passages.

Step 3: Interaction

1. Divide into groups of four and discuss the following questions.

   a. Which, if any, of the problems identified above are apparent in the church today? Are Paul's solutions still applicable?

   b. What new problems about gifts are you aware of in today's church? What solutions would you propose?

   c. What percentage of people in your church would you guess are knowingly using their spiritual gifts in ministry inside or outside the church? Is this a problem? Explain.

2. After recombining as one large group again, share ideas arising out of the small group discussion as your leader posts them on the overhead projector.

Step 4: Exploring Individual Gifts

1. **Wisdom**—The special Spirit-given ability to see situations and issues from God's perspective and to apply God-given insights to specific areas of need.

   1 Corinthians 12:8 To one there is given through the Spirit the message of wisdom.

   a. **The basic idea—**

   b. **Jesus especially modeled this gift—**

c. **Wisdom as a role—**

b. **Much needed in the church today—**

2. **Knowledge**—The special Spirit-given ability to receive from God knowledge that is crucial to ministry and that could not have been obtained in other ways.

   1 Corinthians 12:8 To one there is given through the Spirit . . . the message of knowledge.

   a. **The basic idea—**

   b. **Not just intellectual knowledge—**

   c. **Knowledge as a role—**

3. **Discernment**—The special Spirit-given ability to know whether a certain word, action, or motive has its source in God, sinful flesh, or Satan.

   1 Corinthians 12:10 (NCV) The Spirit gives . . . the ability to know the difference between good and evil spirits.

   a. **The basic idea—**

c. **Discernment as a role—**

Personal Application

In prayer, confess to God any failings or misuse of gifts in the church that you are aware of. Give thanks for the warnings and guidelines of Scripture that will help the church to guard its use of gifts. Ask God to help us understand and use gifts in a way that glorifies him.

After the Session

Read For Added Insight at the end of this session material. Also study about the gifts of wisdom, knowledge, and discernment in the Gift Studies section of this manual. Doing the brief Bible study at the end of each gift study will deepen your understanding of the gift. Be especially attentive when studying the gifts you may have.

Preparation for Session 5

You'll need to plan ahead for session 5. Complete the questionnaires on temperament, ministry passions, skills/talents, spiritual maturity, and availability in Part B—Assessment Forms in this manual. During the next session you'll have an opportunity to share the results of your work on these questionnaires.

FOR ADDED INSIGHT

What should we know about the misuse of spiritual gifts?

Almost every gift can be abused. Spiritual gifts are no exception. Here are four ways in which spiritual gifts sometimes are misused in the church:

- **Gift glorification.** In certain parts of the Christian community today the possession of certain spiritual gifts brings glory to a person. In some charismatic communities, for example, the manifestational gifts (such as miracles, healing, and tongue-speaking) are the most highly prized. People with these gifts are considered to be the most outstanding Christians. In more institutional churches leadership gifts are often the most highly prized because of the prestige they carry.

  Glorifying certain gifts results in a two-level Christianity in which some gifted members become "special" while others not possessing the same gifts are disregarded. This leads to pride in some and inferiority feelings in others. Paul sternly warned the Corinthian church against exalting certain gifts (1 Corinthians 12-14).

- **Gift projection.** Christians who think their particular gifts are the most important sometimes project these gifts outward in such a way that others may feel ashamed and inferior if they don't have them. Peter Wagner calls this the "gift projection syndrome" (*Your Spiritual Gifts Can Help Your Church Grow*). This is what happened in Corinth (1 Corinthians 12:14-20).

- **Gift denigration.** When a gifted person is put down in the church, spiritual gifts are being abused in yet another way. Overly confident, overly independent members of the body may fail to see how much they need to be ministered to by the so-called weaker members. Paul counteracts the tendency to say "I don't need you" by reminding us that the parts of the body that seem weaker are actually "indispensable." Those whom we think are less honorable are worthy of "greater honor." God, he says, has made these adjustments in the body so that we may "have equal concern for each other." (See 1 Corinthians 12:21-25.)

- **Gift individualization.** This is the tendency to over-individualize spiritual gifts. Gifts are given to individuals, but they are given within the context of the Christian community. They are not meant for private use. They are given so that the body of Christ may be edified. In *The Problem of Wineskins,* Howard A. Snyder writes, "The Biblical conception is that the community of believers acts as the controlling context for the exercise of gifts, thus discouraging individualistic aberrations. And gifts must operate in this way. The Church is, to use Gordon Cosby's phrase, 'a gift-evoking, gift-bearing community.' And when the church really functions in this way, the various gifts not only reinforce each other, they also act as check-and-balance to prevent extremes."

Scripture repeatedly emphasizes that gifts are "for the common good." They are to be used "so that the body of Christ may be built up until we all reach unity in the faith and in the knowledge of the Son of God and become mature, attaining to the whole measure of the fullness of Christ" (Ephesians 4:12-13). Paul speaks not of a maturity in isolation but of a maturity in community.

What hinders the introduction of gift-consciousness into the church?

The effort to reintroduce gift-consciousness into the church may be met with some resistance. Here are some barriers that will have to come down if the church is to be gift-oriented:

- **Confusion and suspicion.** There is still much confusion and suspicion about spiritual gifts in the church today. Some churches associate them with charismatic groups. Manifestational gifts (such as miracles, healing, and tongue-speaking) are highly valued by some but feared by others. Still others react to gift-consciousness out of fear that women discovering leadership gifts will demand leadership offices. In the face of confusion and suspicion some will feel more comfortable doing nothing.

- **An institutionalized model.** An institution can function for a time with human organization and natural aptitude. To the extent that the church has learned to depend on its structures, natural abilities, rules, and regulations, it will find difficulty in functioning as an organism dependent on the Holy Spirit's ordering of spiritual gifts. To say that the old institutionalized forms are inadequate amounts to a challenge of the status quo.

- **A consumer mentality.** Many are content simply to attend church events in order to receive something. They are consumers. They pay their dues and get their spiritual uplift in small doses. The pastor is the performer and they are spectators. This arrangement must be altered to allow all members of the body to function as important contributors to the body's life.

- **Lack of community.** The church that is merely a collection of individuals and not a true community will not view gifts as important. Genuine appreciation of spiritual gifts comes when the church recognizes how essential the gifts are for nurturing its community—ministering to and with each other—and for reaching out to the surrounding community for Christ.

Why has there been so little emphasis in the past on spiritual gifts?

A great deal of silence, ignorance, and confusion has persisted on the subject of spiritual gifts. Splinter groups periodically overemphasized certain spiritual gifts. Mainline churches mostly ignored them. Three major factors have significantly affected the church's thinking about spiritual gifts:

- **Institutionalism.** Prior to the sixteenth century Reformation, the church was equated with institution. Certain gifts became associated with the clergy. Other gifts, finding no expression in particular offices of the church, were completely discounted. Church members, who relied on clergy to do the work of ministry, became passive and uninvolved. Though the Reformation corrected many of the abuses of the institutionalized church, it did not go far enough in reclaiming the rightful role and office of member.

- **Rationalism.** The liberalizing trends of the eighteenth century played down the supernatural elements of the Christian faith. Spiritual gifts were naturalized and equated with natural aptitudes and talents. Spiritual gift ministries were considered no different from other activities.

- **Emotionalism.** One reaction to the rationalistic tendency was the pietistic movement of the late eighteenth century. This movement focused attention chiefly on the emotional aspects of spiritual gifts. As a result, the experience of the gifted person was misunderstood as more important than the ministry performed.

GIFTS AND GOD'S OTHER GRACES

Opening Prayer

Preview

In this session we will

- compare spiritual gifts to talents, fruit, filling, and sealing.

- learn how temperament, ministry passions, skills/talents, spiritual maturity, and availability affect our ministry choices.

- explore the spiritual gifts of healing, miracles, and faith.

Step 1: Warm-up Exercise

Working individually, answer the following questions:

1. Spiritual gifts differ from natural talents in that . . . (circle one)

   a. spiritual gifts belong only to believers, not to unbelievers.

   b. spiritual gifts are exceptional abilities while natural talents are ordinary abilities.

   c. spiritual gifts are significant abilities used in ministry. Natural talents are Spirit-given abilities used in a wide variety of activities which, though valid for a Christian to be involved in, are not necessarily ministries.

   d. all of the above

2. Which of the following are true statements concerning the relationship of spiritual gifts and the fruit of the Spirit (Galatians 5:22-23) in the believer? (circle the true statements)

   a. Christians can possess all the fruit, but only some of the gifts.

   b. Christians should possess all of the gifts and some of the fruit.

   c. The fruit is spiritual virtue; the gifts are Spirit-given abilities.

   d. The fruit is temporary; the gifts are eternal.

   e. Gifts without fruit are not worth much.

3. The Bible's message on church offices (for example, elder and deacon) in relation to gifts is that . . . (circle one)

   a. elders must have the gift of administration; deacons, the gift of mercy.

   b. it is chiefly the officebearers of the church who have special abilities called "spiritual gifts."

   c. persons with significant gifts should be ordained to a church office.

   d. none of the above

When everyone has finished, review your answers together.

Step 2: Bible Discovery

Working in groups of three, read and discuss the following Bible passages. Use the questions as discussion starters.

1. **Fruit**

   Galatians 5:22-23 The *fruit* of the Spirit is love, joy, peace, patience, kindness, goodness, faithfulness, gentleness and self-control. Against such things there is no law.

   a. How does the fruit of the Spirit differ from the gifts of the Spirit?

   b. How are fruit and gifts related? (See 1 Corinthians 13:1-3.)

2. **Filling**

   Acts 4:31 After they prayed, the place where they were meeting was shaken. And they were all *filled* with the Holy Spirit and spoke the word of God boldly.

   Ephesians 5:18 Do not get drunk on wine, which leads to debauchery. Instead, be *filled* with the Spirit.

   a. How would you distinguish the gifts of the Spirit from the filling of the Spirit?

b. How are gifts and filling related?

3. Sealing

Ephesians 1:13-14 You also were included in Christ when you heard the word of truth, the gospel of your salvation. Having believed, you were marked in him with a *seal*, the promised Holy Spirit, who is a deposit guaranteeing our inheritance until the redemption of those who are God's possession.

a. Compare and contrast the sealing of the Holy Spirit with the gifts of the Holy Spirit.

Review your answers together as a group. Make sure you understand the distinctions and relationships before moving on.

Step 3: Interaction

1. Reassemble in the same groups of three. Use the following questions to share with each other the results of your assessment forms on temperament, ministry passions, skills/talents, spiritual maturity, and availability.

   a. **Temperament.** What four temperament qualities characterize you?

   b. **Ministry Passions.** What do you think your passions are?

   c. **Skills/Talents.** What two or three dominant skills or talents have you listed?

   d. **Spiritual Maturity.** Where do you rate yourself on the scale of spiritual maturity?

   e. **Availability.** What is your general commitment level? How much time are you willing to give weekly for ministry?

2. Gather again as a whole group and discuss the following questions.

   a. What impressed you as you heard others report the results of their assessment forms? What surprised you?

b. What benefit do you see in these assessments? What danger?

c. What questions do you have about what you have learned?

Step 4: Exploring Individual Gifts

1. **Healing**—The special Spirit-given ability to serve as an instrument through whom God brings physical, emotional, and spiritual healing in an extraordinary way.

   1 Corinthians 12:9 To another [is given] gifts of healing by that one Spirit.

   a. **The basic idea—**

   b. **The purpose of healing gifts—**

   c. **The necessity of medical personnel—**

   d. **Healing as a role—**

2. **Miracles**—The special Spirit-given ability to serve as an instrument through whom God performs extraordinary works as an expression of his presence and power.

   1 Corinthians 12:10 To another [is given] miraculous powers.

   a. **The basic idea**—

   b. **The purpose of miracles**—

   c. **The Western worldview tends to exclude miracles**—

3. **Faith**—The special Spirit-given ability to know with certainty that God wills to do something and is certain to do it, in response to prayer, even when there is no concrete evidence.

   1 Corinthians 12:9 To another [is given] faith by the same Spirit.

   a. **The basic idea**—

   b. **Distinguished from saving faith**—

c. **A gift of great value to the church**—

d. **Faith as a role**—

Personal Application

Praise God that he is living and active in our world today. Thank him for the temperament, ministry passions, skills/talents, spiritual maturity, and availability he has given you. Ask him to combine your gifts with the other graces of God in your life for an effective ministry. Commit all your ways to him.

After the Session

Read For Added Insight at the end of this session. Do the brief studies on the gifts of healing, miracles, and faith in Part C of this manual. As you study individual gifts, put extra effort into exploring the gifts you have discovered as your own.

FOR ADDED INSIGHT

We human beings are very complex creatures. Many factors influence our ministry decisions. Spiritual gifts establish a direction when choosing a ministry; but factors such as ministry passions, skills/talents, and temperament further define the choice. For example, a woman with a teaching gift should choose a teaching ministry, but whether she chooses to teach small children, teenagers, or adults may depend on her ministry passions or her intense area of interest. An introvert with the gift of evangelism will probably choose a different style of evangelistic ministry than an extrovert with the same gift.

This session has invited us to look more closely at five factors that affect our choices: temperament, ministry passions, skills/talents, spiritual maturity, and availability. We call these factors "graces" in recognition of the fact that they are all gifts from God, even though they do not warrant the title "spiritual gifts."

How do spiritual gifts differ from natural talents?

Spiritual gifts and natural talents are alike in several ways. Both are given by God. Both are possessed by believers. Both can be used for the glory of God. But they are not the same. When the apostle Paul describes spiritual gifts, he speaks of abilities that build up the church and advance the cause of Christ. There are also natural abilities that we use in such activities as exploring God's world, earning a living, or developing a hobby. Such activities, though not without significance for the church and the kingdom, may better be classified under the broader mandate of subduing the earth (Genesis 1:28).

Gifts and talents are often finely interwoven within the same person. In *I Believe in the Holy Spirit*, Michael Green writes, "The charismatic gifts are nothing other than the gifts of God's love. They begin with our redemption. They include the heightening of qualities already present or latent within us, such as the gift of administration, leadership, teaching, marriage, or celibacy. These natural qualities can be *charismata* [spiritual gifts] if, and so long as, they are dedicated to the service of the Lord and the building up of his people in the strength that he gives. If they are used selfishly, they can be disastrous."

How are spiritual gifts different from the fruit of the Spirit?

The fruit of the Spirit are virtues, meant to be part of each Christian's life. They are "love, joy, peace, patience, kindness, goodness, faithfulness, gentleness and self-control" (Galatians 5:22-23). Spiritual gifts, on the other hand, are abilities for service. While each Christian should possess all the fruit of the Spirit, he or she will possess only some of the spiritual gifts.

The Bible counts the fruit as greater than the gifts. After mentioning various gifts in 1 Corinthians 12, Paul writes, "And now I will show you the most excellent way" (v. 31). He is referring to the way of love. Without love—one of the fruit—gifts are "but a resounding gong or a clanging cymbal" (1 Corinthians 13:1). And while gifts are temporary, fruit is eternal. The gifts will pass away, but the fruit of love never ends (1 Corinthians 13:8).

How do spiritual gifts differ from offices in the church?

Offices in the church such as minister, elder, and deacon are positions to which the church elects and ordains some gifted members for the purpose of performing official ministries. They serve to build up the people of God and to keep them in fellowship with their Lord. In addition, office-bearers help spiritually gifted members function effectively in ministry. They train members to develop their gifts. (See Ephesians 4:12.) Elders are also "responsible for [our] souls" (Hebrews 13:17, NCV).

While the offices of the church belong to some members; spiritual gifts belong to all. In some circles the responsibility of all believers to serve is called the office of the believer.

No essential difference exists between the ministries of gifted members of the church and the ministries of office-bearers. The distinction is one of function, not of essence. All Christians minister by means of spiritual gifts. All represent Christ, and all function with some measure of Christ's power and authority.

Aren't all Christians to do what gifted Christians do with spiritual gifts?

In many cases the Bible commands us all to do what the spiritually gifted person is doing when using a gift. All Christians are commanded to give generously, to be merciful, to have faith, and to pray. However, some Christians have the spiritual gift of giving, others have the spiritual gift of mercy, and still others have the spiritual gifts of faith and intercession. We all have responsibilities in each area of service, whether we have the specific gift or not. No Christian is excused from serving God in any area of basic Christian responsibility.

It is helpful to distinguish, as Peter Wagner does, between *spiritual gifts* and *roles*. If one has a spiritual gift, he or she is called to exercise that gift to a greater-than-average degree. For example, if a person has the gift of intercession, the gift itself is a challenge to spend more time in prayer than most fellow believers. But all have the *role* of intercession. A person with the gift of mercy is called to a ministry of mercy, while others not having the gift are called to show mercy but are not expected to develop a ministry. For them, mercy is a *role*.

THE GIFTED COMMUNITY

Opening Prayer

Divide into prayer groups of three persons each for your opening prayer time.

Preview

In this session we will

- see the church as a gifted community that is united, mobilized, and advancing by means of gift ministries.

- grow to understand how worship, education, evangelism, service, and stewardship are affected by "gift-consciousness."

- explore the spiritual gifts of tongues, interpretation of tongues, and prophecy.

Step 1: Bible Discovery

1. Remaining in your groups of three, read the following Bible passages and answer the questions. Note that the apostle Paul always places his discussion of spiritual gifts within the context of the body of Christ.

   1 Corinthians 12:25-26 25There should be no division in the body, but . . . its parts should have equal concern for each other. 26If one part suffers, every part suffers with it; if one part is honored, every part rejoices with it.

   How is the body of Christ benefited by the variety of gifts?

   1 Corinthians 14:3-4, 24-25 (NCV) 3Those who prophesy are speaking to people to give them strength, encouragement, and comfort. 4The ones who speak in different languages are helping only themselves, but those who prophesy are helping the whole church. . . . 24But suppose everyone is prophesying and some people come in who do not believe or do not understand. If everyone is prophesying, their sin will be shown to them, and they will be judged by all that they hear. 25The secret things in their hearts will be made known. So they will bow down and worship God saying, "Truly, God is with you."

How does the gift of prophecy benefit the church? How does this gift help a church's evangelistic efforts?

Romans 12:4-5 4Just as each of us has one body with many members, and these members do not all have the same function, 5so in Christ we who are many form one body, and each member belongs to all the others.

How do gifts help the church function? What are the relational benefits?

Ephesians 4:11-13 11It was [Christ] who gave some to be apostles, some to be prophets, some to be evangelists, and some to be pastors and teachers, 12to prepare God's people for works of service, so that the body of Christ may be built up 13until we all reach unity in the faith and in the knowledge of the Son of God and become mature, attaining to the whole measure of the fullness of Christ.

What are the positive benefits to the church as spiritually gifted leaders use their gifts?

Romans 15:18-19 18I will not venture to speak of anything except what Christ has accomplished through me in leading the Gentiles to obey God by what I have said and done— 19by the power of signs and miracles, through the power of the Spirit. So from Jerusalem all the way around to

Illyricum, I have fully proclaimed the gospel of Christ.

What happened in the church as the apostle Paul exercised powerful manifestational gifts (signs and miracles)? Could the same thing happen in the church today?

1 Peter 4:10-11 (NCV) [10]Each of you has received a gift to use to serve others. Be good servants of God's various gifts of grace. [11]Anyone who speaks should speak words from God. Anyone who serves should serve with the strength God gives so that in everything God will be praised through Jesus Christ. Power and glory belong to him forever and ever. Amen.

Who is helped when gifts are used in the church? Who receives the glory?

2. Gather again as one large group and review this Bible Discovery exercise by sharing your answers and asking additional questions you might have.

Step 2: Interaction

Howard Snyder, in *The Problem of Wineskins,* writes,

The church truly becomes the church only when the biblical meaning of spiritual gifts is recovered. A church whose life and ministry is not built upon the exercise of spiritual gifts is biblically a contradiction in terms.

Use Snyder's quote as a springboard to help you begin a discussion of the following questions.

- If a church's life and ministry are built on gifts, how do you think gift discovery and development affect the church's worship? Educational ministries? Outreach efforts? Acts of mercy?

- What problems do you think arise in a church that lacks a gift-consciousness?

- How do you think gift-consciousness affects a church's organizational structures?

- What action, if any, would you like to see your church take regarding spiritual gifts and ministries?

Step 3: Exploring Individual Gifts

1. **Speaking in tongues**—The special Spirit-given ability to speak in sounds and utterances previously unknown to the speaker.

   1 Corinthians 12:10 To another [is given] speaking in different kinds of tongues.

   a. **The basic idea—**

   b. **Valuable but also potentially problematic—**

c. **Cautions to keep in mind—**

2. **Interpretation of tongues—**The special Spirit-given ability to interpret into known language a message spoken in tongues.

   1 Corinthians 12:10 To still another [is given] the interpretation of tongues.

   a. **The basic idea—**

   b. **Necessity and value of interpretation of tongues—**

3. **Prophecy—**The special Spirit-given ability to receive and communicate a message from God so that believers may be edified and encouraged and so that unbelievers may be convinced.

   1 Corinthians 12:10 To another [is given] prophecy.

   a. **The basic idea—**

   b. **A most valuable gift—**

c. **Prophecies need to be tested—**

d. **Prophecy as a role—**

Personal Application

Give thanks for the church, a gifted community, whose ministries extend the work of Christ. Give thanks for other gifted members of the body of Christ and for the ministries God has given them. Make a commitment to develop and use your gifts for the sake of your church. Pray that your church may be equipped, built up, unified, and effective in ministry through the power of the Holy Spirit.

After the Session

Read the section For Added Insight at the end of this session. Do the studies on the gifts of tongues, interpretation of tongues, and prophecy found in the Gift Studies section of this manual. Be sure to study those gifts that you have identified as your own.

FOR ADDED INSIGHT

The church is the body of Christ. Its members are mutually interdependent, caring for each other. Christ, its head, directs all the activities of the church. The life-giving Holy Spirit permeates all its parts. The body expresses the fullness of Christ, who "fills everything in every way" (Ephesians 1:23).

The church needs spiritual gifts to reach its full potential as a life-sharing body. Since its life is expressed through gifted members ministering to one another, the absence of gifts and interdependent ministries signals the absence of body life. In *The Problem of Wineskins,* Howard Snyder underscores the need for proper regard of spiritual gifts in the church:

> The urgent need today is that spiritual gifts be seen and understood in the context of ecclesiology, as in the New Testament. A biblical understanding of spiritual gifts is absolutely essential for a biblical conception of the church. . . . When spiritual gifts are misunderstood—through being individualized, denied, divorced from community, or otherwise distorted—it is the church which suffers. The church truly becomes the church only when the biblical meaning of spiritual gifts is recovered. A church whose life and ministry is not built upon the exercise of spiritual gifts is biblically a contradiction in terms.

How will the gift-conscious church benefit from this emphasis?

First, the church will awaken and mobilize. Frozen assets will thaw. The church's unemployment problem will be solved. Stagnant congregations will come to life as each member begins to seek a rightful place in the community of Christ. The church will gain in spiritual life and health.

Second, a heightened awareness of gifts will assure the church of better leadership. Pastors will be called and/or assigned on the basis of their gifts. Local congregations will be encouraged to choose officebearers on the basis of spiritual gifts. Leaders, functioning by the Spirit's power in the ministries for which they are gifted, will do their work well.

Third, a new spirit of unity will come to the church. In Ephesians 4 the apostle Paul declares that unity and Christlike maturity will result as equipped saints carry on the work of ministry. Few members will feel inferior or unnecessary once they realize that they are vital parts of the body of Christ. Members will develop a greater appreciation for one another as they recognize their mutual interdependence. Pursuit of programs, methods, and organizational objectives will become subservient to the pursuit of ministries flowing out of love.

Fourth, churches will be strengthened in evangelism as outreach-oriented gifts are developed. And if, in addition, gifts of hospitality and shepherding function well, new members will find their way into the body, and the church will grow.

What happens when a church ignores spiritual gifts?

If a church does not help its people discover, develop, and use spiritual gifts, it will suffer from the following problems:

- **An inactive, uninvolved membership.** An *inactive church member* is really a contradiction in terms. Membership in the true church equates with involvement in the ministries necessary to the life of the body. A church that is not gift-conscious is perpetuating the lie that one can truly be a member of the church of Christ by simply attending and "paying the dues." Not so.

- **An overworked minority.** The church that slights the doctrine of spiritual gifts will have to rely on a minority to do its work. That minority, including the pastor, will soon feel overworked, resulting in burnout and neglect of even the most essential tasks. Such a church is like a passenger ship—the crew does all the work while the passengers enjoy the ride. The New Testament model is more like a merchant ship, on which everyone is part of the crew and everyone has a job to do.

- **An unsatisfied communal life.** Without the functioning of gifts, there is no healthy communal life. Some churches that love to sing "Blest be the tie that binds our hearts in Christian love" don't really know what that means. Their members do not talk about real problems and hurts or "bear one another's burdens," for few know the real burdens of others. It is comfortable, in a way, to be part of such a congregation. But it's not very satisfying.

- **A lack of conversion growth.** Any church indifferent to spiritual gifts will not need to worry about much conversion growth. Without the crucial gifts of evangelism, the church will win few converts. Further, those few who are converted through the church's ministries are not likely to stay in a church that lacks the gift of hospitality. And converts are not likely to grow if discipling gifts are not exercised.

- **Overdependence on programs.** If few members have ministries that flow from spiritual giftedness, the church will need to depend on programs to meet basic needs. But programs always flop unless they are staffed by gifted, obedient people.

How does gift-consciousness affect the church's structure?

The following changes can become a reality when a church begins to think seriously about spiritual gifts:

- **Selectivity in ministry assignments.** Most ministries in the church require selectivity. Not everyone should serve as a greeter, or go calling in the community, or take a turn in an office. The simple truth is that not everyone can do everything equally well. Thinking seriously about gifts will help the church avoid an "everyone-ought-to" mentality.

- **Opportunities for togetherness.** If gifts are to function well, the church needs to provide opportunities for members of the congregation to communicate freely with one another. Members cannot minister to one another or coordinate their efforts unless they get to know each other. Small groups, one of many structures that encourage informal and free exchange, help facilitate openness. Howard Snyder writes in *The Problem of Wineskins,* "Without the small group, the church in urban society simply does not experience one of the most basic essentials of the Gospels—true, rich, deep Christian soul fellowship, or *koinonia.*"

- **Ministry teams.** It is often helpful for a gifted person to develop a ministry with a group of people having related gifts and ministries. The church that provides ministry teams, task forces, or action groups actively encourages the use of gifts for ministry.

How do spiritual gifts help Christians minister outside the church?

The ministries of the church extend not only to those on the membership rolls but also to people and institutions outside. The presence of Christ is not limited to the sanctuary—nor are the gifts he has given to his people. It's in the world that the church must live out its life, use its spiritual gifts, and make an impact for Christ.

Persons, groups, and institutions in the world are all objects of God's concern. The world, too, is called to give account to Jesus Christ as Lord. It needs to hear the good news of God's salvation and to be reshaped by the Holy Spirit's transforming power. As the body of Christ in the world, the church is the bearer of this good news. The church itself is evidence that Christ cares for the world, and in the midst of the world the church is to be a spiritually gifted, loving, and ministering organism.

EMPOWERED FOR MINISTRY

Opening Prayer

Preview

In this session we will

- discover from Scripture the link between gifts and ministry.

- understand the need for empowerment as a precondition to exercising gifts.

- explore the spiritual gifts of giving, hospitality, and intercession.

Step 1: Warm-up Exercise

In groups of three,

- share one way in which you have used a gift or ability God has given you in ministry.

- identify a spiritually gifted person in your church and describe the ministry he or she is engaged in.

Step 2: Bible Discovery

1. When we accept Jesus as our Savior and Lord, the Holy Spirit comes to live within us to transform our lives and to empower us for ministry. But the power of the Spirit becomes active in and through our ministry experiences only when we ask for it in faith and act on it in obedience. This empowerment is referred to in Scripture as baptism in (or with) the Holy Spirit, as receiving the Holy Spirit, as having the Holy Spirit fall upon us, or as being filled with the Holy Spirit. This experience belongs potentially to all believers but in reality only to those who act in faith and obedience.

   While we are saved by grace "through faith . . . not by works," we are also "created [anew] in Christ Jesus to do good works" (Ephesians 2:8-10; 2 Corinthians 5:17). In other words, we are called to respond to God's grace through obedient living. And we can do this only by the transforming empowerment of the Holy Spirit (2 Corinthians 3:18). We have to give ourselves up so that the Spirit can use us for ministry (Ephesians 4:22-24, 30).

Individually, read the following Scripture passages and answer the questions.

   John 14:12-14 (NCV) [12]"I tell you the truth, whoever believes in me will do the same things that I do. Those who believe will do even greater things than these, because I am going to the Father. [13]And if you ask for anything in my name,

I will do it for you so that the Father's glory will be shown through the Son. [14]If you ask me for anything in my name, I will do it."

   What precondition does Jesus set for doing works similar to the works he did? What is Jesus' role in these works? What is the end result?

   Luke 24:48-49 [48]"You are witnesses of these things. [49]I am going to send you what my Father has promised; but stay in the city until you have been clothed with power from on high."

   Acts 1:8 "You will receive power when the Holy Spirit comes on you; and you will be my witnesses in Jerusalem, and in all Judea and Samaria, and to the ends of the earth."

   What, according to these verses, is required before becoming a witness for Christ?

   John 20:21-22 [21]Jesus said, "Peace be with you! As the Father has sent me, I am sending you." [22]And with that he breathed on them and said, "Receive the Holy Spirit."

   How did Jesus prepare his disciples to accomplish the mission task to which he sent them?

   Acts 1:4-5 [4]On one occasion, while he was eating with them, [Jesus] gave them this command: "Do not leave Jerusalem, but wait for the gift my Father promised, which you have heard me speak about. [5]For John baptized with water, but in a few days you will be baptized with the Holy Spirit."

What was needed before Jesus' disciples launched into their life callings?

1 Corinthians 2:14 (NCV) A person who does not have the Spirit does not accept the truths that come from the Spirit of God. That person thinks they are foolish and cannot understand them, because they can only be judged to be true by the Spirit.

Who is unable to receive gifts of the Spirit of God? Why?

Now that you've looked through these Scripture passages and answered the questions, identify the one thing that is necessary for powerful and effective ministry. How can that become a reality?

2. Review your answers as a group. Identify central themes and discuss any remaining questions you may have.

Step 3: Action Plan

1. Complete the following action plan individually.

   a. Considering all the gifts God has given me, what does he want me to do for him

   • in my relationships with friends, at home, or at work?

   • in the church?

• in the community?

b. What will help me do these things? What might hinder me?

c. Specifically, how can I use my gifts more fully?

2. Gather in groups of three and share your action plan.

Step 4: Exploring Individual Gifts

1. **Giving**—The special Spirit-given ability to contribute personal and material resources to the Lord's work freely, cheerfully, and sacrificially.

   Romans 12:8 (NCV) Whoever has the gift of giving to others should give freely.

   a. **The basic idea—**

   b. **The amount is not the issue—**

c. **Giving as a role—**

2. **Hospitality**—The special Spirit-given ability to love, welcome, and graciously serve guests and strangers so that they feel at home.

   1 Peter 4:9 Offer hospitality to one another without grumbling.

   a. **The basic idea—**

   b. **God himself models hospitality—**

   c. **Hospitality as a role—**

3. **Intercession**—The special Spirit-given ability to pray faithfully and effectively for others for extended periods and to see many specific answers to those prayers.

   Colossians 4:12 Epaphras . . . is always wrestling in prayer for you.

   a. **The basic idea—**

b. **Biblical models of intercession—**

c. **Intercession involves a way of life—**

d. **Intercession as a role—**

Personal Application

Praise God for "his incomparably great power for us who believe" (Ephesians 1:19). Thank him that his power is available to all of us who claim it through faith and obedience. Ask the Lord Jesus Christ to baptize you with his Spirit and with power so that you may be equipped to serve him with strength. Seek his guidance in your life and ministry.

After the Session

Read For Added Insight at the end of this session. Complete the Gifts Studies section on the spiritual gifts of giving, hospitality, and intercession.

Before leaving this session, make arrangements to meet individually or in pairs with one or two spiritual-gift consultants from your church. They will lead you through the process of matching your gifts, temperament, ministry passion, skills/talents, spiritual maturity, and availability with the right ministry. To prepare for this, do the following:

a. Set a meeting time with a consultant.

b. Complete the Ministry Resumé at the end of Part B—Assessment Forms in this manual, and take the resumé with you to the interview.

c. Thank God for your Spirit-given gifts. Confess any failure in the past to use spiritual gifts or to engage in ministry. Ask for the Spirit's guidance in locating a proper ministry, and dedicate yourself wholly to minister in line with God's will.

FOR ADDED INSIGHT

By now you should have a strong sense of what your spiritual gifts are. The fact that you possess a gift is a call from Christ to use it. Muscles are useless unless they are flexed. Spiritual gifts are useless until they are put to work in the service of the King. They are instruments for ministry, not ornaments for display.

The use of gifts begins by dedicating them to the Lord, expressing our willingness to serve God with our spiritual capacities. We must say sincerely, "Here I am, Lord; use me and my abilities." Paul invites us to present our "bodies as living sacrifices" (Romans 12:1) in the context of using our spiritual gifts.

Development follows dedication. Development occurs with use. That's why Paul says in Romans 12:6 that we are to use our different gifts "according to the grace given us" and "in proportion to [our] faith." Faithful use of a gift increases its effectiveness and value. Here are some intentional ways in which spiritual gifts can be developed:

- **Begin by studying Scripture.** Study passages that relate particularly to your gifts. Study the lives of biblical characters who exercised gifts like yours. Study the roles related to your gifts.

- **Read books and articles** that expand your thinking in the area of your own spiritual gifts.

- **Talk to other Christians** who have similar gifts. They may be your best source of understanding your gifts. Learn what they have done with their gifts, what ministries they have developed, and what resources were most helpful to them.

- **Attend conferences, seminars, workshops, and classes** that will help you cultivate your gifts. Christians spend many hours in leisure-time classes and activities. Why not spend time in courses that aid gift development? If you can't get to a seminar because of distance or cost, it may be available on audio- or videocassette.

Don't be satisfied just to discover your gifts. Grow and mature in your gift abilities as you grow in spiritual maturity.

What can a spiritually gifted person do to find a ministry?

Don't wait to be asked to get involved in a ministry. Following are specific ways to discover or develop a ministry.

- **Pray for guidance and strength.** Ask for strength to do what God calls you to do. Trying to operate in one's own strength is a great sin. As you begin to exercise your spiritual gifts, remember what Jesus said in John 15:5: "Apart from me you can do nothing." Ask God for guidance in knowing when, where, and how he wants to use your gifts.

- **Be sensitive to the needs of others.** Pray for eyes to see needs that are both near and real. Look beneath the surface of people's lives to see the hurts that cry out for healing. Try to meet some of the needs you discover. Spiritual gifts are the Holy Spirit's provisions for meeting human needs.

- **Focus your efforts in the area of your gifts.** Learn to say no to things that are not in line with your gifts. Get out of unfruitful activities. Establish priorities that will allow you time to develop a ministry. Then begin to use your gifts.

- **Be willing to begin small.** If, for example, you think you have the gift of evangelism, begin by seriously using it with just one other person. Or work alongside someone who is similarly gifted. If you have the gift of teaching, you may want to begin by sitting in on a church school class and observing the teacher.

- **Be yourself.** Remember that you are a unique person with an equally unique mix of gifts. Don't try to imitate anyone else. Your way of serving is probably God's best for you.

- **Be prepared to give yourself.** Jesus' threefold requirement for discipleship—"Deny yourself, take up your cross, and follow me" (see Matthew 16:24)—applies also to exercising your gifts. Howard Snyder clearly focuses the issue of giving ourselves:

  > Ministry is not determined exclusively by personal desire, but by the cross. . . . As one is crucified with Christ and dies to his own will, the Holy Spirit resurrects within him his significant gift. So the spiritual gift, rightly exercised, is not self-centered; it is self-giving.

  > But we must go further than this and say that a Christian discovers the true meaning of the crucifixion as he really begins to exercise his gift. Faithful ministry of the gift of the Spirit will lead him into depths of self-giving he never dreamed possible—and God planned it that way. This is the way we are created—psychologically, emotionally, and spiritually.

  —*The Problem of Wineskins*, p. 136

A Christian who wants to be "carried to the skies on flowery beds of ease" will never "win the prize" and never know the joy of serving the Lord with spiritual gifts.

How can a church help its members develop spiritual gifts?

A church can do many things to help its people discover, develop, and use spiritual gifts for ministry:

- **Organize for ministry.** Take a fresh look at the structures of your church and ask, "Just how much real ministry is happening within the structures?" and "How are the structures helping people to minister?" Leaders in the churches need to see themselves as servants whose task is to help people develop ministries.

- **Recruit along gift lines.** Unfortunately many church members serve where they do because they did not dare to say no or because "somebody had to do it." A church can help its people develop gifts by assigning its gifted members to ministries that fit their gifts.

- **Equip for ministry.** "To prepare God's people for works of service" (Ephesians 4:12) is not simply a matter of theological training or on-the-job instruction. Rather, this equipping should help a person develop spiritual gifts and the ministries related to them.

- **Provide support.** God does not intend for us to minister in isolation. Spiritually gifted church members need to find personal support as they engage in ministry. By providing a healthy support structure, the church can facilitate gift ministries.

- **Be conscious of needs in the home, church, and community.** Since spiritual gifts are given to meet needs, the church that helps its members become more conscious of needs will also encourage the use of gifts. Awareness of needs may also lead to the development of new ministries designed to meet those needs.

- **Affirm spiritual gifts.** All gifts and gifted members are important. Church leaders who affirm this in words and actions will help members develop self-esteem and confidence in service.

A Final Word

Discovering the Bible's teachings about gifts is one of the most uplifting experiences a Christian can have. Accepting and using our gifts brings great joy and power (see 1 Thessalonians 1:5-6). Spiritually gifted Christians, though weak in themselves, find their strength in the Lord (Philippians 4:13). May you know the joy and experience the power of God's Spirit working in you and through you to do his good will as you discover and use your spiritual gifts.

ASSESSMENT FORMS

Part B

SPIRITUAL GIFT DISCOVERY QUESTIONNAIRE

About the Questionnaire

As you complete this questionnaire, remember that questionnaires have their limits. This questionnaire will help you discover your gifts, but its results must be considered only tentative. You may not actually have the gifts you identify as yours. Gifts tentatively identified need to be confirmed by others and used successfully in ministry before you can be sure they are really yours.

This questionnaire distinguishes between *working gifts* and *waiting gifts.* A working gift is a gift you have used or are currently using in some way. You are able to identify working gifts by answering questions aimed at your past or present ministry activities. A waiting gift is a gift which you have not used in ministry but which is waiting to be developed. Even though you have not used a waiting gift, there will be hints of it in your daily living. Waiting gifts can be identified by answering questions related to interests, inclinations, sensitivities, attitudes, and concerns.

Don't be disappointed if you learn that you do not have certain gifts you desire to have. God has gifted others in the body of Christ with the gifts you do not have. The body will not be deprived. Be content with God's distribution of gifts and ministry in the church. Thank him for the wonderful and unique diversity he has put into his body. Remember that you benefit when other members use their gifts.

How to Complete the Questionnaire

Each statement in the following questionnaire has five possible responses related to how much the statement is true of you: Very Little, Little, Some, Much, Very Much. These represent percentages on a scale of 1-100%, as follows:

Very Little	=	0-20%
Little	=	20-40%
Some	=	40-60%
Much	=	60-80%
Very Much	=	80-100%

Read each statement. Decide to what extent the statement is true of you. Check the appropriate column. Your first impressions are usually correct.

Don't worry if most of your marks are placed toward the right or toward the left. But try to avoid putting too many marks in the middle, or Some, column.

THE FOLLOWING IS TRUE OF ME . . .

		VERY LITTLE	LITTLE	SOME	MUCH	VERY MUCH
1.	I enjoy organizing programs, tasks, and people to achieve an objective.	1	2	3	4	5
2.	I have used my ability in music, acting, visual arts, or graphics arts to benefit the body of Christ.	1	2	3	4	5
3.	I can usually discern whether a person's words, actions, or motives are godly, fleshly, or from the evil one.	1	2	3	4	5
4.	I regularly minister to others by offering practical counsel and guidance for their spiritual growth.	1	2	3	4	5
5.	I enjoy talking about Christ to those who don't know him, and I usually receive a positive response.	1	2	3	4	5
6.	I have had the experience of knowing that God willed to do something and then saw him do it in response to faith and prayer.	1	2	3	4	5
7.	I enjoy sharing the financial resources God has shared with me.	1	2	3	4	5
8.	I know that God heals supernaturally, and I have seen him do so.	1	2	3	4	5
9.	I like to provide hospitality for guests and do not feel imposed upon by unexpected visitors.	1	2	3	4	5
10.	I enjoy praying for the needs of others and do so regularly.	1	2	3	4	5
11.	I sense what God is saying when I hear someone speak in tongues.	1	2	3	4	5
12.	I can distinguish my own thoughts from knowledge I have received from the Spirit.	1	2	3	4	5
13.	God, at times, gives me a vision for a task that attracts others to get involved.	1	2	3	4	5
14.	I feel deeply for hurting people and often am able to turn compassion into practical, cheerful help.	1	2	3	4	5
15.	I am confident that God can and does work miracles today because I have seen them.	1	2	3	4	5
16.	With a message from God I have pleaded the cause of God to the people of God.	1	2	3	4	5
17.	I enjoy doing tasks that help others serve more effectively.	1	2	3	4	5
18.	I enjoy taking responsibility for the spiritual well-being of others who were helped to grow spiritually through my assistance.	1	2	3	4	5
19.	Content comes alive for students (children or adults) when I teach.	1	2	3	4	5
20.	I pray in an unknown language at various times.	1	2	3	4	5
21.	I often give people practical insights that help to solve problems.	1	2	3	4	5
22.	I like to make things more orderly.	1	2	3	4	5
23.	I enjoy expressing myself creatively for God through music, drama, poetry, visual arts, or graphic arts.	1	2	3	4	5

#	Statement	VERY LITTLE	LITTLE	SOME	MUCH	VERY MUCH
24.	It disturbs me when false teachings and false practices creep into the church.	1	2	3	4	5
25.	I suffer along with hurting, troubled, and discouraged people and want to help them see God's answers to life's problems.	1	2	3	4	5
26.	I desire to share my faith with others.	1	2	3	4	5
27.	I find myself taking God's promises and applying them to given situations without doubt.	1	2	3	4	5
28.	I am easily moved to give when I become aware of need or opportunity in people's lives or in God's kingdom.	1	2	3	4	5
29.	A deep compassion for the sick often motivates me to pray for their healing.	1	2	3	4	5
30.	I am sensitive to offer small acts of kindness that make a difference for guests or strangers.	1	2	3	4	5
31.	I am sensitive to the prayer needs of others and desire to give them prayer support.	1	2	3	4	5
32.	I am drawn to worship services in which tongues are not unusual, and I have a heightened sense that God is speaking to us through tongues.	1	2	3	4	5
33.	I regularly receive impressions that I believe come from the Holy Spirit.	1	2	3	4	5
34.	I am able to present the vision for a task in a manner that attracts others to get involved.	1	2	3	4	5
35.	I find myself drawn to hurting people, and I desire to help them.	1	2	3	4	5
36.	I sense specific instances when a miraculous display of God's power would strengthen our faith.	1	2	3	4	5
37.	I receive spiritual insights from the Word and/or Spirit concerning people and issues, and I desire to express those insights.	1	2	3	4	5
38.	I sense when others need a helping hand, and I am ready to give it.	1	2	3	4	5
39.	My desire to see spiritual growth in believers leads to a willingness to be personally involved in nurturing and discipling ministries.	1	2	3	4	5
40.	I have a strong desire to communicate truths and/or information that will help believers (young or old) to grow in the faith.	1	2	3	4	5
41.	I delight in being open to the supernatural influence of the Holy Spirit, and I allow him to take over my tongue.	1	2	3	4	5
42.	I sometimes have extraordinary, God-given insights into situations, but I am not given to express these insights.	1	2	3	4	5
43.	I am able to design and execute effective plans to accomplish goals.	1	2	3	4	5
44.	I have special music, drama, writing, painting, or sculpting skills that I like to use in God's kingdom.	1	2	3	4	5
45.	I detect phoniness or false teachings in situations where others are swayed and misled.	1	2	3	4	5

	VERY LITTLE	LITTLE	SOME	MUCH	VERY MUCH
46. People in the Christian community have been spurred on to love and good works by my counsel and encouragement.	1	2	3	4	5
47. I have been instrumental in leading others to believe in Christ as their Savior.	1	2	3	4	5
48. In certain cases I have a conviction that God would do what seemed unlikely.	1	2	3	4	5
49. I give cheerfully and liberally in support of the Lord's work, often above the average.	1	2	3	4	5
50. I pray expectantly for persons who are physically, emotionally, or spiritually ill.	1	2	3	4	5
51. I have a knack for making strangers feel at ease in my home and at church.	1	2	3	4	5
52. I agonize over and identify with others as I pray for them.	1	2	3	4	5
53. Believers gathered in public worship have been edified by my interpretations of tongues.	1	2	3	4	5
54. God has revealed to me knowledge of things that would happen before they actually came to pass.	1	2	3	4	5
55. God has used me to motivate others who have willingly followed and worked together in a kingdom project.	1	2	3	4	5
56. I regularly enjoy helping those who suffer physical, mental, or emotional problems.	1	2	3	4	5
57. God has used me to demonstrate his miraculous power in a situation in which natural means were not sufficient.	1	2	3	4	5
58. God is using me to build up and encourage other Christians by speaking to them of spiritual things.	1	2	3	4	5
59. I willingly do menial tasks that help build up the body of Christ.	1	2	3	4	5
60. I am able to provide ongoing care, spiritual nourishment, and protection to other believers.	1	2	3	4	5
61. I find that I communicate truth clearly and effectively in such a way that others (children or adults) learn.	1	2	3	4	5
62. I am being built up in the faith when I use the gift of tongues.	1	2	3	4	5
63. God gives me insights in situations in which I had no previous knowledge.	1	2	3	4	5
64. I would enjoy giving direction to a church ministry.	1	2	3	4	5
65. I think I could be very creative in music/arts/drama/writing, and I am open for ways to develop this ability.	1	2	3	4	5
66. I tend to perceive when hidden motives are present for people's words or behaviors.	1	2	3	4	5
67. I believe that counsel and instruction from the Word will help people grow to spiritual maturity.	1	2	3	4	5

		VERY LITTLE	LITTLE	SOME	MUCH	VERY MUCH
		1	2	3	4	5
68.	I have a burden for friends and acquaintances who do not know Jesus Christ.	1	2	3	4	5
69.	I sense occasions when the "prayer of faith" is needed.	1	2	3	4	5
70.	I am willing to make personal sacrifices and to maintain a lower standard of living in order to benefit God's work.	1	2	3	4	5
71.	I am drawn to ministries that offer care and healing to hurting persons.	1	2	3	4	5
72.	I tend to be more aware of the needs of guests than of my own needs.	1	2	3	4	5
73.	At times I am motivated to pray by an inner conviction that God does things in response to prayer that he wouldn't do otherwise.	1	2	3	4	5
74.	An interpretation I received from the Spirit was confirmed when someone more experienced in tongue-interpretation gave publicly the very interpretation I had received.	1	2	3	4	5
75.	When talking with a troubled person, I sometimes discern the previously undetected root hurt without being told.	1	2	3	4	5
76.	I have a sense for motivating and directing others in a project.	1	2	3	4	5
77.	The sight of misery always makes me want to find a way to express God's love to those who suffer.	1	2	3	4	5
78.	I get excited that God "is able to do immeasurably more than all we ask or imagine" (Ephesians 3:20), and I believe that he wants to demonstrate his power through me.	1	2	3	4	5
79.	I am strongly motivated to declare the truth as God has revealed it to me.	1	2	3	4	5
80.	I like to serve, and sometimes I take the initiative to meet needs.	1	2	3	4	5
81.	I sense a deep pastoral concern when I know of Christians who need spiritual counsel.	1	2	3	4	5
82.	I am motivated to get involved when there is an obvious need for knowledge or insight.	1	2	3	4	5
83.	I sometimes feel a flow of life and love within me that transcends the rational.	1	2	3	4	5
84.	I enjoy seeing spiritual knowledge applied in real-life situations.	1	2	3	4	5
85.	In a leadership role I am able to motivate, delegate, and coordinate effectively.	1	2	3	4	5
86.	I have communicated biblical truth in visual, graphic, dramatic, or artistic ways.	1	2	3	4	5
87.	I have developed an ability to distinguish between truth and error in the spiritual realm.	1	2	3	4	5
88.	I am excited at the potential I see in people, and I often encourage them in order to bring out the best in them.	1	2	3	4	5

		VERY LITTLE	LITTLE	SOME	MUCH	VERY MUCH
89.	I'm flexible and adaptable. I become all things to all people in order to win some.	1	2	3	4	5
90.	At times I expect God to intervene in supernatural ways in spite of evidence to the contrary.	1	2	3	4	5
91.	I take a personal interest in the causes and people I support, both financially and in ministry.	1	2	3	4	5
92.	People have experienced healing as a result of my ministry with them.	1	2	3	4	5
93.	My home is always open to those in need of hospitality.	1	2	3	4	5
94.	I am conscious of ministering to others as I pray for them, releasing God's power and grace in their lives.	1	2	3	4	5
95.	I have spoken in tongues and have also received an interpretation.	1	2	3	4	5
96.	I sometimes experience God-given, supernatural insights when I am in prayer.	1	2	3	4	5
97.	I have served effectively as a leader by setting clear goals and by involving people in working toward these goals.	1	2	3	4	5
98.	I am effective in ministering to hurting people who often attest to the blessing they have received.	1	2	3	4	5
99.	I was God's instrument in opposing Satan's work in a specific way through God's mighty power.	1	2	3	4	5
100.	God has used me to proclaim timely and urgent messages that have come to me through his Word and/or Spirit.	1	2	3	4	5
101.	I find practical ways of helping others, and I gain satisfaction from doing this.	1	2	3	4	5
102.	The Lord uses me to watch over and guide other Christians toward spiritual maturity.	1	2	3	4	5
103.	I usually know what it takes to hold the interest of those I teach.	1	2	3	4	5
104.	Sometimes I am so caught up in wonder and love for God that I pray in the Spirit.	1	2	3	4	5
105.	I am able to apply spiritual knowledge in practical ways.	1	2	3	4	5
106.	I have a sense for how and when a project or ministry needs to be better organized.	1	2	3	4	5
107.	I am drawn to people with creative abilities, and I see them as persons who model what I want to be and do.	1	2	3	4	5
108.	I perceive when people pretend to be what they are not.	1	2	3	4	5
109.	I am glad when someone who needs comfort, consolation, encouragement, or counsel seeks my help.	1	2	3	4	5
110.	I seek relationships with non-Christians and enjoy helping them come to know the Lord.	1	2	3	4	5
111.	I find it easy to believe that "mountains are moved" by faith.	1	2	3	4	5

		VERY LITTLE	LITTLE	SOME	MUCH	VERY MUCH
112.	I see money and possessions as tools to serve God, and I regularly set them aside for this purpose.	1	2	3	4	5
113.	I am aware that God has given me a healing touch that needs to be more fully developed.	1	2	3	4	5
114.	I have a genuine appreciation for each person to whom I minister.	1	2	3	4	5
115.	I am trying to intercede regularly for those in ministry to advance the Lord's work.	1	2	3	4	5
116.	I am sensitive to nudges from the Holy Spirit.	1	2	3	4	5
117.	I sometimes know things without knowing how I came to know them.	1	2	3	4	5
118.	I am quick to sense when a group is spinning its wheels for lack of leadership, and I want to take charge.	1	2	3	4	5
119.	Kindness and compassion are so much a lifestyle for me that needy persons are attracted to me.	1	2	3	4	5
120.	When I sense a need or concern, I tend to imagine God working a powerful miracle to solve the problem.	1	2	3	4	5
121.	I am convinced that God wants me to speak out for him on social and moral issues of the day.	1	2	3	4	5
122.	I am usually able to identify needs, and I don't mind offering help.	1	2	3	4	5
123.	I like being with other Christians and am willing to be involved if they need counsel or guidance.	1	2	3	4	5
124.	I get excited about new ideas I can share with others.	1	2	3	4	5
125.	In expressing praise to God, I sometimes come to the point where cognitive speech no longer conveys the meaning.	1	2	3	4	5
126.	I often know what to do, how to do it, and when to do it in situations that leave others puzzled.	1	2	3	4	5

KEY CHART

How to Use the Key Chart

Complete this key chart on your own after completing the preceding questionnaire. Begin by reading the following instructions carefully.

1. Place the number 1, 2, 3, 4, or 5, which you have assigned to each of the 126 statements in the questionnaire, next to the corresponding number in this chart.

2. Add each row of three numbers in the Working-Gift Chart and the Waiting-Gift Chart across to the right, and write the sum in the Total box on the right side of each chart.

3. Circle the four highest scores in the Working-Gift Chart Total column and write the names of these gifts in the box at the bottom titled My Working Gifts. List the highest numbers first. In case of a tie, give the higher rating to the gift that has the highest combined score for both waiting and working gifts.

4. Next look at the Waiting-Gift Chart Total column. Circle the four highest scores in this column that were not identified as working gifts. Write these gifts in the box entitled My Waiting Gifts, again listing the highest numbers first. Break any ties as you did in number 3 above.

   Remember that although the remaining gifts may not be your spiritual gifts, you still have a responsibility in each of these areas.

KEY CHART

Spiritual Gift	Working-Gift Chart			TOTAL	Waiting-Gift Chart			TOTAL
Administration	1	43	85		22	64	106	
Creative Ability	2	44	86		23	65	107	
Discernment	3	45	87		24	66	108	
Encouragement	4	46	88		25	67	109	
Evangelism	5	47	89		26	68	110	
Faith	6	48	90		27	69	111	
Giving	7	49	91		28	70	112	
Healing	8	50	92		29	71	113	
Hospitality	9	51	93		30	72	114	
Intercession	10	52	94		31	73	115	
Interpretation of Tongues	11	53	95		32	74	116	
Knowledge	12	54	96		33	75	117	
Leadership	13	55	97		34	76	118	
Mercy	14	56	98		35	77	119	
Miracles	15	57	99		36	78	120	
Prophecy	16	58	100		37	79	121	
Service	17	59	101		38	80	122	
Shepherding	18	60	102		39	81	123	
Teaching	19	61	103		40	82	124	
Tongues	20	62	104		41	83	125	
Wisdom	21	63	105		42	84	126	

My Working Gifts

Highest scored gift	
2nd	
3rd	
4th	

My Waiting Gifts

Highest scored gift	
2nd	
3rd	
4th	

Transfer your three highest working gifts and your two highest waiting gifts to your Ministry Resumé at the end of this section.

TEMPERAMENT ASSESSMENT FORM

This section on temperament contains a series of questions that will help you understand and identify the traits that form your temperament. It also contains brief explanations of eight basic temperament traits.

Temperament is defined as "a distinct set of characteristics, given by God, that are reflected in how I relate to others and respond to the world around me. My temperament distinguishes my spiritual gifts and makes my service uniquely valuable" (*Discovery*, an unpublished course on spiritual gifts).

There are four basic temperament categories, each with two choices. A person is either extroverted or introverted; sensing or intuitive; thinking or feeling; and judging or perceiving. These eight basic traits were first identified by psychologist Carl Jung. Later, psychologists Katherine Briggs and her daughter Isabel Myers created a questionnaire based on these categories to help people identify their temperament traits. This test has become known as the Myers-Briggs Type Indicator (MBTI). The following temperament assessment form uses Jung's basic categories and is based on the MBTI but is much briefer. This simplified test will probably be adequate for most ministry-placement purposes in the local church. However, those wishing to go more deeply into temperament analysis are encouraged to secure a MBTI from Consulting Psychologists Press, Inc., 3803 E. Bayshore Road, Palo Alto, CA 94303. *Please Understand Me* by David Keirsey and Marilyn Bates (Prometheus Nemesis Books, 1978) is another excellent resource for more extensive study of temperament traits. It, too, is based on the eight basic traits mentioned above.

Some things to remember as you complete this test and consider the results:

1. **There are no right or wrong answers.** There are no right or wrong temperaments. Temperaments just are. Your answers will simply help you know yourself better. This knowledge will help you accept both your strengths and weaknesses, understand and relate more comfortably to others, and make better choices.

2. **You're not locked into traits.** If one trait is dominant in you, that doesn't mean its opposite is inoperative. It simply means that the dominant trait is part of your usual way of looking at and deciding things. However, that "usual way" is reversible. Introverts can reach out. Extroverts can look inward. Thinkers can be warm-hearted; feelers can be coolheaded. Don't let yourself become imbalanced. Explore the poles.

3. **Sin can and does affect temperament traits.** While temperaments are neither right or wrong, what we do with them can be right or wrong. Each personality type has its potential for usefulness and for abuse. Exaggerated traits may become instruments of evil. Underdeveloped traits may contribute to failure. Seek the filling of God's Spirit in order to increase your strengths and minimize your weaknesses. Let God work through your temperaments to accomplish his purposes.

4. **Temperaments need to be taken into consideration as you choose a ministry in the kingdom.** You will serve more comfortably and effectively if your ministry fits your temperament as well as your abilities.

Directions

This assessment form contains a series of items that answer a lead question. In each case there are two statements representing two temperament traits. Between them are six numbers. First decide whether the statement on the right or the left fits you better; then decide on the degree to which it is true of you. For example, if the right-hand statement fits you better, circle one of the numbers on the right side. Notice that in the numbering system, 3 is "very strongly tends," and 1 is "somewhat tends." The six numbers have the following meaning:

◄ In this direction	In this direction ►
Very strongly tends 3	3 Very strongly tends
Definitely tends 2	2 Definitely tends
Somewhat tends 1	1 Somewhat tends

On your first pass through the assessment form, concentrate on circling your responses to all the statements. Then make a second pass to add up the circled numbers and to write the totals in the boxes at the bottom of each paired section. For example, if you have marked a 1, a 3, and two 2s on the right side, the total on that side would be 8. The total on the other side would be 0. The temperament trait with the highest number most characterizes you. Write the name of that trait on the line beneath each section. In case of a tie, pick the one that you think most characterizes you.

1. Where do I tend to focus my attention?

	Extroversion (focus is on outer world)							Introversion (focus is on inner world)
1	I tend to be energized by having people around.	3	2	1	1	2	3	I tend to be energized in solitary activities, drained by having too many people around.
2	I tend to feel lonely without people around.	3	2	1	1	2	3	I tend to feel lonely in a crowd.
3	I like to have many relationships.	3	2	1	1	2	3	I prefer a limited number of relationships.
4	I like variety and action in my work environment.	3	2	1	1	2	3	I like quiet places where I can work alone and concentrate.
	Total							Total

My dominant temperament trait in this category is _____.

2. How do I find out about things?

	Sensing (relies on senses to secure information)							Intuition (goes beyond senses to secure information)
5	I tend to focus on information and facts in a situation.	3	2	1	1	2	3	I tend to seek beyond information to meanings, relationships, and possibilities.
6	I like to work with practical, here-and-now realities.	3	2	1	1	2	3	I would rather focus on how things can be improved in the future.
7	I prefer to deal with proven procedures.	3	2	1	1	2	3	I prefer to do it my own way.
8	I tend to look at what is actually happening.	3	2	1	1	2	3	I tend to look for new possibilities.
	Total							Total

My dominant temperament trait in this category is _____.

3. How do I make decisions?

	Thinking (relies on thoughts and ideas)						Feeling (relies on feelings)
9	I tend to make decisions by analyzing situations and weighing evidence.	3 2 1		1 2 3			I tend to make decisions by responding to people and what they value.
10	I am prone to be coolheaded.	3 2 1		1 2 3			I am prone to be warmhearted.
11	I value consistency of thought.	3 2 1		1 2 3			I value consistency of harmonious human relationships.
12	I am good at arguing.	3 2 1		1 2 3			I am good at peacemaking.
	Total						Total

My dominant temperament trait in this category is _____.

4. How do I orient to the outer world?

	Judging (prefers planned orderly world)						Perceiving (prefers flexible spontaneous world)
13	I feel an urgency until a decision is made.	3 2 1		1 2 3			I feel a hesitancy when a decision needs to be made.
14	I like to have things under control.	3 2 1		1 2 3			I don't mind operating with loose ends.
15	I tend to want things settled and finished.	3 2 1		1 2 3			I tend to want things open-ended.
16	I like it when things are well organized.	3 2 1		1 2 3			I prefer an adapt-as-you-go approach.
	Total						Total

My dominant temperament trait in this category is _____.

Write below the four temperament traits that characterize you; then transfer them to the Ministry Resumé at the end of this section. Finish by reading the descriptions of those four traits on the following page.

_____   _____

_____   _____

Trait Descriptions

Extroversion. Extroverts tend to focus on the outer world. They are energized by having people around, and they experience loneliness when they are not in contact with people. They prefer having many relationships. They tend to prefer variety and action over solitary quietness. Three-quarters of the general population are extroverts.

Introversion. Introverts tend to focus on the inner world. They are energized by solitary activities and drained by having many people to deal with. They prefer a limited number of relationships. They tend to like quiet places where they can work alone. One-quarter of the population fit this category.

Sensing. Sensation-preferring persons rely on their senses to acquire information. They are grounded in the facts and prefer working with practical, here-and-now realities. They tend to orient to what actually has happened rather than to what might happen. About 75 percent of the population have this trait.

Intuition. Intuitive persons deal comfortably in the realms of meanings, relationships, and possibilities—realms that go beyond sensing. They are prone to focus on how things can or should be rather than how things are. They are possibility thinkers whose thoughts take them into the future. About 25 percent of the population are intuitive.

Thinking. Thinking-preference persons tend to rely on thoughts and ideas to make decisions. They decide on the basis of objective criteria discerned through analysis. They like dealing with principles and policies and ordinarily are coolheaded and good at argumentation. Slightly more men than women possess this trait.

Feeling. Feeling-preference persons tend to rely on feelings in making decisions. They decide on the basis of the impact their decision has on themselves and others. They like dealing with people and ordinarily are warmhearted and good at peacemaking. Slightly more women than men have this trait.

Judging. Don't mistake this word to mean "judgmental." It refers to those who, in orienting to the outer world, prefer to make a judgment or come to a conclusion. Coming to closure is more important to them than becoming aware. They tend to want things settled, and they feel a sense of urgency until a decision is reached. They usually like to have things well organized.

Perceiving. Perceivers tend to look rather than decide. Becoming aware is more important to them than coming to closure. They tend to be hesitant when a decision needs to be made, and they prefer to leave things more open-ended. They like things to be flexible and are more comfortable with "adapt-as-you-go" than with lots of up-front planning.

MINISTRY-PASSION ASSESSMENT FORM

God has given you particular spiritual gifts and temperaments that uniquely equip you for service. He has probably also placed within you a certain yearning to make a difference in a particular area—a concern for a specific human need in an area of increased interest. This is your ministry passion.

Your ministry passion is God's way of pulling you toward a particular area of ministry. You will be most effective and fulfilled in ministry if you apply your spiritual gifts to an area in which you have a strong desire to make a difference.

In order to find clues to your ministry passion, you need to think about things and activities that excite you. What areas most interest you? What do you think is the most important problem that needs to be addressed? The following questions are designed to help you discover your ministry passion.

1. Which of the following areas do you like working in the most?

   _____ Things (carpentry, sewing, etc.)

   _____ Information, Ideas

   _____ People

   _____ Other

2. Which of the following groups of people do you like working with the best? For which do you have the greatest concern?

   _____ Infants   _____ Children

   _____ Teens   _____ Young Adults

   _____ Adults   _____ Singles

   _____ Couples   _____ Elderly

   _____ Other

3. In which of the following areas do you have the strongest feeling that things should be changed? (This is not an exhaustive list but simply an attempt to stimulate your thinking.)

   _____ Poverty   _____ Hunger

   _____ Ecological Issues   _____ Crime

   _____ Drug/Alcohol Abuse   _____ Illiteracy

   _____ Health Care   _____ Physical Disabilities

   _____ Doctrinal Issues   _____ AIDS

   _____ Emotional Distress   _____ Ethical Issues

   _____ Crisis Pregnancies   _____ Care of the Elderly

   _____ Learning Disabilities _____ Family Problems

   _____ Generation Gaps   _____ Spiritual Lostness

   _____ Spiritual Immaturity

   _____ Other

4. Which of the following ministry areas in your church are you most interested in?

   _____ Worship   _____ Education/Discipling

   _____ Evangelism   _____ Caring

   _____ Enfolding   _____ Communications/ Marketing

   _____ Stewardship   _____ World Missions

5. If money, time, family, or education were not an issue, and you knew you could not fail, what would you do for Christ and his kingdom?

6. After reflecting on your answers to these questions, what ministry passion(s) do you think you have?

   a. _____

   b. _____

   c. _____

Transfer your responses in 6a and 6b to your Ministry Resumé at the end of this section.

This material is adapted from *Discovery,* an unpublished gift-discovery course developed by David Armstrong, Kevin Blair, Robert Boomsma, Barbara Brouwer, Brenda Cook, Karen Folkerts, and Judy Stremler of Elmhurst Christian Reformed Church, Elmhurst, Illinois. Used by permission.

SKILLS/TALENTS ASSESSMENT FORM

In addition to spiritual gifts, God has given you skills and talents to perform specific tasks. You may have been born with these or developed them through life experiences. It is God's will that you use your talents and skills as well as every aspect of your life to his honor and glory. As you seek your place of service in his kingdom, consider your special talents and skills. God's work will be accomplished more effectively and you will feel more comfortable and productive in service if you are using your talents.

List below your skills and talents. In what areas do you feel most proficient and confident? Here are some examples to help you think: music, carpentry, math, sewing, art, cooking, computer programming, landscaping, medicine, counseling, writing, mechanics, accounting, law, engineering, public relations, advertising, aerobics, painting, electrical work, library, drama, sound systems, building maintenance, coaching, typing, filing. Keep these in mind as you determine where God is leading you. Go beyond this list if you can.

a. _____

b. _____

c. _____

d. _____

Transfer a, b, and c to your Ministry Resumé at the end of this section.

This material is adapted from *Discovery*, an unpublished gift-discovery course.

SPIRITUAL MATURITY ASSESSMENT FORM

It is important to realize that the level of spiritual maturity you have attained will affect the type of service you will be able to give to Christ and his church. Therefore, in order to understand yourself better, you need to assess your level of spiritual maturity honestly and accurately.

Spiritual Maturity Levels

Read the following paragraphs describing three levels of spiritual maturity. Which do you think most accurately describes you?

_____ **A new/young Christian** is in the early stages of learning what it means to be a Christian. This Christian may be a recent convert *or* someone who has known the Lord for a while but is only in the early stages of developing a truly Christian lifestyle. This person is excited about the possibilities of a life with Christ but needs to learn more about the Christian faith and how to apply it to daily life.

_____ **A stable/growing Christian** has matured to the point of stability and consistency. This person trusts God, has a clear understanding of his will for life, and has made a good start in using spiritual disciplines.

_____ **A leading/guiding Christian** has matured greatly in Christ and has attained a high degree of faithfulness in the Christian walk. This person has a deep trust in God that is evident to others. He or she provides a clear model of Christlikeness, and by word and example tends to lead other Christians into a deeper relationship with Christ.

Adapted from *The Lost Art of Disciple Making* by William Shell and Leroy Eims (Zondervan/NavPress, 1978), and from *Network* by Bruce Bugbee, Don Cousins, and Bill Hybels (Willow Creek Community Church, 1990).

Spiritual Maturity Characteristics

The Bible reveals a number of characteristics that Christians should pursue. The following list is adapted from *Essentials of Discipleship* by Francis Cosgrove (NavPress, 1980), and *Come Follow Me* by William Shell (Great Commission Publications, 1988).

For each of the eleven characteristics of a Christian, rate yourself on a scale of 1 to 4 with 1=never evident, 2=rarely evident, 3=sometimes evident, and 4=usually evident.

Rating	Characteristic
_____	I put Christ first.
_____	I am committed to a life of purity.
_____	I have a daily devotional time and a developing prayer life.
_____	I desire to learn and apply the Word of God.
_____	I am a learner, open and teachable.
_____	I regularly attend church and am involved.
_____	I desire fellowship with other Christians.
_____	I am developing and using spiritual gifts.
_____	I demonstrate a servant attitude.
_____	I am faithful in giving.
_____	I am active in evangelism.

On a scale of 1 to 10 (with 10 being high) what would you say is your level of spiritual maturity? Take into account the ratings you made in the exercise above.

1   2   3   4   5   6   7   8   9   10   (circle one)

Transfer your responses to your Ministry Resumé at the end of this section.

This material is adapted from *Discovery*, an unpublished gift-discovery course.

AVAILABILITY ASSESSMENT FORM

As you have worked through the preceding assessment forms, you will have developed some sense of how God is calling you. Now you must consider your priorities and determine how much time you are willing and able to commit to a ministry in the church.

General Commitment Level

The first thing to ask yourself is this: "How much of a commitment can I or do I want to make?" Look at the categories below. Which of these fits you?

My commitment level is . . .

_____ Light: generally uncommitted or unavailable

_____ Moderate: somewhat committed or available

_____ Strong: committed; significant time is available

_____ Major: highly committed; major schedule changes are possible

Assessment of Personal Schedule

About how much time each week do you think you should spend in each of the following areas? There are 168 hours per week. Usually about 60 hours are spent sleeping. That leaves 108 hours for other activities.

1. Work hours? _____ (includes housework, shopping, yard work, home upkeep, etc.)

2. Family activities? _____ (includes family meals, family leisure time, etc.)

3. Personal time? _____ (includes projects, personal devotion time, entertainment, etc.)

4. Volunteer time? _____ (includes church and other organizations)

How much time on a weekly basis would you be willing and able to spend in a church-related ministry?

_____ hours

Additional Comments

Transfer your responses to your Ministry Resumé at the end of this section.

This material is adapted from *Discovery,* an unpublished gift-discovery course.

MINISTRY RESUMÉ

Name _____

After completing each part of this section, enter your personal responses into the following chart. All together these will help you decide on the type of service God has designed for you.

1. Spiritual Gifts Key Chart

Highest working gifts:

a. _____

b. _____

c. _____

Highest waiting gifts:

a. _____

b. _____

2. Temperament

My four temperament traits are:

a. _____

b. _____

c. _____

d. _____

3. Ministry Passions

I have a strong desire to work in the following areas:

a. _____

b. _____

4. Skills/Talents

In addition to my spiritual gifts, God has given me the following skills/talents:

a. _____

b. _____

c. _____

5. Spiritual Maturity

a. My spiritual maturity level is _____.

b. On a scale of 1-10 I rate myself at about _____.

6. Availability

After assessing all of my priorities, I can describe my availability as follows:

a. My commitment level is (circle one):

    light   moderate   strong   major

b. I believe I can spend _____ hours in ministry each week.

> Please provide a copy of this resumé to your church's gift consultant before your placement interview.

GIFT STUDIES

Part C

ADMINISTRATION

Definition

The special Spirit-given ability to design and execute a plan of action through which a number of believers are enabled to work effectively together to do the Lord's work.

Administration as a Spiritual Gift

The gift of administration is identified in 1 Corinthians 12:28. The Greek word for administration—*kubernasis*—means "one who guides or directs toward a goal." It was commonly used to identify the one who steers or pilots a ship. An able pilot had the ability to keep the ship and crew sailing smoothly to the next port. The word was also used to describe the manager of a household. As a spiritual gift, administration has to do with a God-given ability to guide the affairs of the kingdom of God. The person with this gift brings organizational and management skills to the body of Christ.

This gift is also called the gift of organization. But this does not necessarily mean the administrator has a neat desk and well-organized files. Rather, the administrator is a *people* organizer. In the church he or she gives clear guidance to the process of ministry and facilitates the activities of others working toward kingdom goals. The gifted administrator is able to get things done through people by directing, motivating, and coordinating their activities. Nehemiah, for example, was an expert administrator, motivating and harmonizing the activities of thousands of people as they rebuilt the walls of Jerusalem.

The gift of administration mentioned in 1 Corinthians 12:28 must be distinguished from the gift of leadership (Romans 12:8). The two are related yet different. The leader sees the future and sets the goals; the administrator devises the plans to accomplish the goals. The leader knows where the port is; the administrator knows how to navigate the ship into the port. The leader holds out the vision; the administrator helps to translate the vision into reality by developing a plan of action and directing other believers involved in the process. While the gifts of administration and leadership are different, it is not uncommon for one person to have both gifts.

The gift of administration can be used in many different ways. A person with this gift will usually take an organized approach to daily activities such as personal devotions, time management, and family life. In the life of the church he or she will be a model committee member, coordinator, director, superintendent, or planner. On a board this person will provide valuable insights into managing a system and achieving goals.

Characteristics of the Spiritually Gifted Administrator

If this is a working gift for me,

- I am able to organize ideas, tasks, people, and time to achieve an objective.
- I am able to make effective plans to achieve goals.
- I have a sense for delegating important tasks to the right people at the right time.

If this is a waiting gift for me,

- I like to help plan things in which people are involved.
- I would enjoy giving direction to a church ministry.
- I have a sense for how and when projects or ministries need to be better organized.
- I am a good decision maker and problem solver.

Ways to Use the Gift of Administration

Personal/informal uses:

- organize family devotions
- help a friend develop a family budget
- organize a neighborhood get-together

Ministries within the church:

- oversee the church school
- direct a program
- chair a committee

Community-oriented ministries for Christ:

- organize a fund-raising campaign
- serve on the board of a home for the elderly people
- organize a rally

Potential Liabilities in the Gift of Administration

The spiritually gifted administrator can sometimes tend to

- rely on well-organized plans rather than on the power of the Spirit and on prayer.
- think of projects as more important than people. People get used instead of loved and supported.
- "take over" in such a way as to leave little room for other people's ideas and concerns.
- be too careful and block progress toward an overall vision.

Administration as a Responsibility of All Christians

An administrator devises effective plans and carries them out to accomplish a task. All people are administrators in their own lives. Jesus calls us to plan wisely and effectively. "Store up for yourselves treasures in heaven," he said (Matthew 6:20). He expects Christians to plan their lives well by building on a solid foundation (Matthew 7:24-27). Scripture warns against planning that leaves out the Lord (James 4:13-15).

Discerning the Gift of Administration

1. What inclinations, insights, sensitivities, or concerns have I had that indicate I have the gift of administration?

2. How has God used this gift through me to affect the lives of other people?

3. Have others said things about me that have helped to confirm that I have this gift? If so, what?

4. In what ways could this gift be further used . . .

   a. in my personal relationships at home, with friends, or at work?

   b. in the church?

   c. in community-oriented ministries for Christ?

5. What problems or pitfalls, if any, have I encountered in using this gift?

Exploring Administration from Scripture

1. Write out the part of 1 Corinthians 12:28 that refers to this gift.

2. How does Jethro exercise the gift of administration in Exodus 18:12-27?

3. How does Nehemiah exercise this gift? (See Nehemiah 4:11-13, 16-23.)

4. What does Luke 14:28-30 teach us about the importance of good management?

5. How did the appointment of deacons with administrative gifts help the newly founded Jerusalem church (Acts 6:1-7)?

CREATIVE ABILITY

Definition

The special Spirit-given ability to communicate truth and advance God's kingdom through creative means such as music, drama, visual arts, graphic arts, and writing skills.

Creative Ability as a Spiritual Gift

Some Christians have distinctive creative abilities they are called to use in the service of the King. For example, Bezalel and Oholiab, associates of Moses, were given unique abilities by the Holy Spirit. As Exodus 35:31-35 (NCV) tells us, "The LORD has filled [Bezalel and Oholiab] with the Spirit of God and has given [them] the skill, ability, and knowledge to . . . design pieces to be made of gold, silver, and bronze, to cut stones and jewels and put them in metal, to carve wood, and to do all kinds of work. . . . They can plan and sew designs in the fine linen with the blue, purple, and red thread." God gave these gifts in order to build and beautify the tabernacle and, thereby, to promote centralized worship for the people of God as they traveled to the promised land of Canaan.

Music is a creative ability mentioned in Scripture. David was uniquely gifted as a musician and songwriter (2 Samuel 23:1). His great poetic ability was a particular skill God used to enhance temple worship. David's psalms have blessed the church throughout the ages. Musicians also were specially appointed because of their creative abilities (1 Chronicles 16:41-42; 2 Chronicles 5:12-13; 7:6).

Though this gift is not specifically named in the New Testament as a spiritual gift, it deserves a place in the church today. The church of the New Testament is essentially one with the church of the Old Testament; God is the same yesterday, today, and forever. The Scriptures offer no reason to believe that God has discontinued his practice of giving creative abilities for ministry in the kingdom.

Characteristics of the Person with Creative Ability

If this is a working gift for me,

- I have used a particular creative ability (such as writing, painting, banner making, drama, music, graphic arts, sculpting) to benefit the body of Christ.

- I am able to communicate divine truth visually, graphically, or vocally in interesting, imaginative, and inspiring ways.

- people have been spiritually stimulated and have grown in their appreciation of God and his world through my artistic efforts.

If this is a waiting gift for me,

- I am drawn to people who have the ability to express themselves creatively through music, drama, writing, or the arts and see them as models of what God wants me to be.

- I am creative and often do things on my own to develop my creative abilities, but I have had little opportunity to develop or use them in public settings.

- I sense within me latent creative abilities (in drawing, writing, music, and so on) that I would like to use for the kingdom of God.

Ways to Use the Gift of Creative Ability

Personal/informal uses:

- make music or paint for personal enjoyment
- keep a daily journal or write a family history
- assist a friend in home decoration

Ministries within the church:

- sing in a church group
- design liturgical banners
- lead the craft time in a children's class
- participate in a worship drama

Community-oriented ministries for Christ:

- do freelance writing
- assist in a community arts festival
- act in a dramatic presentation of the life of Christ

Potential Liabilities in the Gift of Creative Ability

A person with this gift can sometimes tend to

- assume the ability is a natural talent and not be concerned to use it for Christ and his kingdom.
- use the ability for self-glory.
- fail to develop the gift because of laziness.
- look down on persons with other gifts.

Creative Ability as a Responsibility of All Christians

We human beings are called to subdue the earth and have dominion over it (Genesis 1:28). This calls for a daily effort by all of God's people to bring creative order to our world. God has given us many natural abilities to accomplish this task. All Christians are called to exercise creative imagination in their daily activities. While God gave special abilities to Bezalel and Oholiab, he also gave skill to all the artisans and designers building the temple (Exodus 31:6; 36:2). Often it's in worship that we have opportunity to give expression to creative abilities. Paul, for example, encourages all believers, "Speak to one another with psalms, hymns, and spiritual songs. Sing and make music in your heart to the Lord" (Ephesians 5:19; see also Colossians 3:16).

Discerning the Gift of Creative Ability

1. What inclinations, insights, sensitivities, or concerns have I had that indicate I have the gift of creative ability?

2. How has God used this gift through me to affect the lives of other people?

3. Have others said things about me that have helped to confirm that I have this gift? If so, what?

4. In what ways might this gift be further used . . .

    a. in my personal relationships at home, with friends, or at work?

    b. in the church?

    c. in community-oriented ministries for Christ?

5. What problems or pitfalls, if any, have I encountered in using this gift?

Exploring Creative Ability from Scripture

1. Read Exodus 31:1-6 and 35:30-35. What distinctive creative abilities did God give to Bezalel and Oholiab?

2. What ability mentioned in Exodus 35:34 enabled them to transmit their knowledge? What was the result (v. 35)?

3. What, in addition to skill, was required of a person involved in the work of building the temple? (See Exodus 36:2.)

4. What place did music and dance have in temple worship? (See Psalm 149:1-4; 150.) What provision was made to insure that worship was led by spiritually gifted leaders? (See 1 Chronicles 15:16-24; 16:41-42.)

5. Why were special musical gifts given, according to 1 Chronicles 25:6-7?

DISCERNMENT

Definition

The special Spirit-given ability to know whether a certain word, action, or motive has its source in God, sinful flesh, or Satan.

Discernment as a Spiritual Gift

Paul speaks of discernment as a spiritual gift, calling it the ability of "distinguishing between spirits" (1 Corinthians 12:10). This phrase suggests a supernatural ability to detect the difference between a message from the Holy Spirit and a message from evil spirits in those who purport to act or speak for God.

Jesus regularly exercised this gift. When Peter opposed his going to Jerusalem to suffer, Jesus discerned the evil source behind his comment and responded, "Get behind me, Satan!" (Matthew 16:23). When Jewish teachers of the law said of Jesus, "This fellow is blaspheming," Jesus, knowing their thoughts, asked, "Why do you entertain evil thoughts in your hearts?" (Matthew 9:3-4).

The apostles also used the gift of discernment. When Ananias and Sapphira tested the early Christian community with their lies, Peter discerned their deceit and pronounced judgment upon them (Acts 5:1-11). When Simon the sorcerer sought the gift of the Holy Spirit for wrong reasons, Peter urged him to repent, seeing that he was "full of bitterness and captive to sin" (Acts 8:9-25). Paul, "filled with the Holy Spirit," discerned the true source of Elymas's opposition to the gospel and said, "You are a child of the devil and an enemy of everything that is right! You are full of all kinds of deceit and trickery" (Acts 13:9-10). Paul also detected and cast out an evil spirit that had possessed a slave girl, whose owners were using her to tell fortunes (Acts 16:16-18).

There is both a natural and a supernatural dimension to discerning. Persons who have this gift will naturally be able to spot motives and attitudes, sniff out hypocrites, and distinguish truth from error, even if these are not directly associated with evil spirits. Many theologians and faithful biblical scholars possess this gift and use it to help protect the church from heresy. But sometimes the gift operates supernaturally as the Holy Spirit gives the discerner, through an inner knowing, awareness of demonic influence in the words, actions, or motives of another person. The awareness may be a mental impression or it may be a feeling which registers in the pit of the stomach or some other part of the body. Discernment often functions in conjunction with gifts of wisdom and knowledge.

The church has always needed this gift. There were many false teachers and prophets seeking to deceive the elect (Matthew 7:15; Mark 13:22). Peter says, "They will secretly introduce destructive heresies," and "many will follow" (2 Peter 2:1-2). Paul warned Timothy of deceiving spirits and things taught by demons (1 Timothy 4:1) and of rulers, authorities, powers of darkness, and spiritual forces of evil with whom we must struggle (Ephesians 6:12). Satan, "the father of lies," is ever seeking to pervert the truth (John 8:44). The gift of discernment is given by the Spirit to help protect the church from those who operate under Satan's influence. Without this gift the church is vulnerable to the attacks of Satan and the poison of false teaching.

The spiritual gift of discernment is essential in the church today. Satan is still sowing seeds of error and untruth. New cults spring up. We are bombarded on every side with untruth. Undiscerning church members are easily misled by false teachers. God safeguards his people by means of the written Word, which stands as an objective standard of truth, and by means of believers who are enabled by the Holy Spirit to discern whether words or actions originate from an evil spirit. Although all believers are to "test everything" (1 Thessalonians 5:21), those with the gift of discernment have a heightened ability and responsibility to do so.

Characteristics of the Person with the Gift of Discernment

If this is a working gift for me,

- I have been able to detect phony persons and false teachings when others have not.

- I have developed an ability to perceive people's true spiritual motivation.

- I am able to tell when a person is controlled or influenced by an evil spirit.

If this is a waiting gift for me,

- I am deeply concerned when I sense that false teachings and false practices are creeping into the church.

- I tend to look beneath the surface to detect hidden sources of words or actions.

- I can usually spot a hypocrite.

Ways to Use the Gift of Discernment

Personal/informal uses:

- warn friends about false teaching

- oppose persons with wrong motives or deceitful purposes

- protect people from the dangers of mass media

Ministries within the church:

- interview people for ministry positions
- evaluate study materials
- engage in spiritual warfare through prayer

Community-oriented ministries for Christ:

- counsel those who have fallen prey to satanic schemes
- discern and encounter evil in societal structures

Potential Liabilities in the Gift of Discernment

A person with this gift can sometimes tend to

- become an overzealous heresy hunter.
- be tempted to have a proud, critical, or judgmental spirit.
- unnecessarily attack and berate people.
- withdraw from the church because it is less than perfect.

Discernment as a Responsibility of All Christians

Many voices clamor to be heard today. Every Christian needs to be discerning. The Holy Spirit gives every believer the capacity to discern good from evil in order to live a life of godliness (Philippians 1:9-11). The psalmist pleads, "I am your servant; give me discernment that I may understand your statutes" (Psalm 119:125). Hebrews 5:14 speaks of this gift as the mark of a mature Christian. John encourages all believers to distinguish between truth and error: "Dear friends, do not believe every spirit, but test the spirits to see whether they are from God, because many false prophets have gone out into the world" (1 John 4:1). In addition, John declares that every believer has "an anointing from the Holy One, and all of you know the truth" (1 John 2:20; see also v. 27). This anointing enables each believer to test the validity of any spiritual teaching (1 Corinthians 2:14-15). Full of the Holy Spirit, believers will increasingly be able to see as Christ sees.

Discerning the Gift of Discernment

1. What inner inclinations, insights, sensitivities, or concerns have I had that indicate I have the gift of discernment?

2. How has God used this gift through me to affect the lives of other people?

3. Have others said things about me that have helped to confirm that I have this gift? If so, what?

4. In what ways might this gift be further used . . .

   a. in my personal relationships at home, with friends, or at work?

   b. in the church?

   c. in community-oriented ministries for Christ?

5. What problems or pitfalls, if any, have I encountered in using this gift?

Exploring Discernment from Scripture

1. Write out the phrase from 1 Corinthians 12:10 that identifies the gift.

2. How is Satan trying to make inroads into the church? (See Ephesians 6:11-12; 2 Corinthians 11:13-15.)

3. According to 2 Peter 2:1-3, how do false teachers work? What effect to they have on the church?

4. How is the church to deal with false spirits and teachers? What is the acid test by which they are measured? How is the spirit of truth known? (See 1 John 4:1-3, 6.)

5. How was the gift of discernment used in each of the following situations? What were the results?

   • Matthew 16:21-23

   • John 2:23-25

   • Acts 5:1-11; 8:18-23

   • Acts 13:6-12; 16:16-18

6. Read Revelation 2:2-6, 14-15, 20. How does Christ regard the church that discerns false teachers and teachings? What about the church that doesn't?

ENCOURAGEMENT

Definition

The special Spirit-given ability to effectively encourage, comfort, challenge, or rebuke others to help them live lives worthy of God.

Encouragement as a Spiritual Gift

Encouragement is identified as a spiritual gift in Romans 12:8. The emphasis of the Greek word *parakaleo* in that passage is fundamentally positive. Even when the connotation is "to rebuke," it means doing so in order to bring about positive change. This Greek term denotes standing alongside another person to encourage, support, or console as well as to challenge, urge, or rebuke, where necessary, for spiritual growth and to "spur one another on toward love and good deeds" (Hebrews 10:24). This gift is sometimes described as "the counseling gift."

Many of the people in the New Testament exercised this gift. Paul and Barnabas strengthened and encouraged "a large number of disciples" to "remain true to the faith" (Acts 14:21-22). In fact, Barnabas, whose name means "Son of Encouragement," encouraged and discipled both Paul and Mark (Acts 4:36; 9:26-28; 11:25-26; 12:25; 13:5; 15:37-39). Peter, commissioned by Jesus to "strengthen" his brothers (Luke 22:32), encouraged the elders of the churches in Asia Minor to be diligent and faithful in their work (1 Peter 5:1-3).

The gift of encouragement can be exercised either privately or publicly. Peter seems to have used the gift while preaching in Jerusalem on Pentecost day and again at Antioch (Acts 2:38-40; 11:23). The apostle Paul urged Timothy to "correct, rebuke, and encourage" by means of preaching (2 Timothy 4:2). Paul himself sometimes used the gift more privately, dealing with "each of" the Thessalonians "as a father deals with his own children, encouraging, comforting and urging [them] to live lives worthy of God" (1 Thessalonians 2:11-12). Paul also urged the Thessalonians to "encourage the timid, help the weak, [and] be patient with everyone" (5:14). The objective of these exhortations is to strengthen Christians for effective service.

The role of the gifted encourager is similar to that of the Holy Spirit, who is also called the "Counselor" or "Comforter" (also "Paraclete"). These names derive from the same root as the word for encouragement (see John 14:16, 26). The third person of the Trinity stands alongside a believer in order to help. So, too, the spiritually gifted encourager, enabled by the indwelling Spirit, becomes a channel for the comfort and counsel of the divine Comforter.

Characteristics of the Person with the Gift of Encouragement

If this is a working gift for me,

- people in the Christian community have been spurred on "to love and good deeds" by my counsel and encouragement, guided by the Holy Spirit.
- I am excited at the potential I see in people, and I often encourage them in order to bring out the best in them.
- I regularly minister to others by offering practical counsel and guidance for their spiritual growth.

If this is a waiting gift for me,

- I identify deeply with hurting people and want to help them experience God's answers to life's problems.
- I believe that counsel and instruction from the Word can help people grow to spiritual maturity.
- I am glad when people who need comfort, encouragement, and counsel seek my help.

Ways to Use the Gift of Encouragement

Personal/informal uses:

- counsel a friend with a problem
- encourage a new Christian
- serve as a spiritual mentor or "soul-mate"

Ministries within the church:

- visit and counsel inactive members
- serve as an inspirational speaker to youth groups
- help other church members find ways to use their gifts in ministry

Community-oriented ministries for Christ:

- serve at an ex-offender contact center
- be a Big Brother or Big Sister
- counsel at a crisis-pregnancy center
- be a telephone-hotline counselor

Potential Liabilities in the Gift of Encouragement

A person with this gift can sometimes tend to

- create inappropriate dependencies by getting too involved in people's lives.

- overextend in counseling people and neglect other important duties.
- be satisfied with easy solutions to complex problems.

Encouragement as a Responsibility of All Christians

All Christians are called to care for and encourage one another. Hebrews 3:13 says, "Encourage one another daily." Paul challenges believers to "encourage one another and build each other up" (1 Thessalonians 5:11). The same kind of responsibility is laid on Christians in Hebrews 10:24-25: "Let us consider how we may spur one another on toward love and good deeds. . . . Let us encourage one another." No one is excused from this responsibility.

Discerning the Gift of Encouragement

1. What inclinations, insights, sensitivities, or concerns have I had that indicate I have the gift of encouragement?

2. How has God used this gift through me to affect the lives of other people?

3. Have others said things about me that have helped to confirm that I have this gift? If so, what?

4. In what ways might this gift be further used . . .

    a. in my personal relationships at home, with friends, or at work?

b. in the church?

c. in community-oriented ministries for Christ?

5. What problems or pitfalls, if any, have I encountered in using this gift?

Exploring Encouragement from Scripture

1. Write out the phrase in Romans 12:8 that identifies the gift of encouragement.

2. What did Paul do with this gift, according to Acts 20:31; 1 Thessalonians 4:10-12; and 5:14-22?

3. How does Hebrews 10:24-25 help us to understand the gift of encouragement?

4. What should be the attitude of one who encourages, according to 1 Thessalonians 2:11-12?

5. What evidence does the Bible give that Barnabas had the gift of encouragement? (See Acts 9:26-28; 11:25-26; 12:25; 13:5; 15:37-39)

6. How does the role of the gifted encourager compare to that of the Holy Spirit?

EVANGELISM

Definition

The special Spirit-given ability to present the gospel to unbelievers in clear and meaningful ways that bring a positive response.

Evangelism as a Spiritual Gift

Evangelism is identified as a gift in Ephesians 4:11, where it is embodied in a person—the evangelist. There are many signs in the New Testament signaling the operation of this gift. Philip was a gifted and effective evangelist (Acts 8:5-40; 21:8). Paul and Barnabas "won a large number of disciples" by exercising their gift of evangelism as they preached the good news in Asia Minor (Acts 14:21). In 2 Timothy 4:5 Paul encourages Timothy the pastor to "do the work of an evangelist."

The objective of the gift of evangelism is to bring unbelievers to faith in Jesus Christ and into the church. This gift, used both in one-to-one situations and in public settings, is also useful in the structure of the local church. According to Paul, the evangelist is to work with others in the church "to prepare God's people for works of service" (Ephesians 4:11-12). This will happen as the evangelistically gifted person serves as an example and trains those who may have yet to discover and develop this spiritual gift. In addition, leaders who have the gift will lift up the vision of outreach. Administrators who have the gift will help to organize evangelistic ministries. Teachers who have the gift will instruct others in evangelism techniques. According to Peter Wagner, 5 to 10 percent of the adult members of a local church are likely to have the gift of evangelism (*Your Spiritual Gifts*, p. 160).

Characteristics of the Spiritually Gifted Evangelist

If this is a working gift for me,

- I enjoy talking about Christ to those who do not know him, and I usually receive a positive response.

- I have been instrumental in leading others to believe in Christ as their Savior.

- I am able, in the Spirit's power, to clearly present the message of salvation to unbelievers.

If this is a waiting gift for me,

- I have a strong desire to share my faith with others.

- I am concerned about friends and acquaintances who do not believe in Christ.

- I am motivated to begin relationships with non-Christians and to help them come to know and love the Lord.

Ways to Use the Gift of Evangelism

Personal/informal uses:

- witness to those who do not know Jesus Christ
- make tactful use of evangelistic tracts
- lead my own children to commitment

Ministries within the church:

- participate in a church visitation program
- lead an evangelistic Bible study
- share the gospel with children in a Bible school setting

Community-oriented ministries for Christ:

- become involved in marketplace ministry
- give an evangelistic message at a rescue mission
- counsel at an evangelistic crusade

Potential Liabilities in the Gift of Evangelism

The spiritually gifted evangelist can sometimes tend to

- rely on one's own power of expression or persuasion to convert people.

- take pride in the number of converts won.

- pass negative judgment on others who don't have the gift.

- be a "scalp hunter" lacking true compassion.

Evangelism as a Responsibility of All Christians

To evangelize is to bring the good news of Christ's salvation to unbelievers. Not all Christians are evangelists, but all believers are called to witness. All Christians whose hearts are in tune with the Father will strongly desire with him, "not wanting anyone to perish," that everyone will "come to repentance" (2 Peter 3:9). All Christians share responsibility to carry out the Great Commission (Matthew 28:18-20). All are involved in bringing the good news "to the ends of the earth" (Acts 1:8). All are also called to "preach the word" whenever and wherever there is opportunity (Acts 8:4).

Discerning the Gift of Evangelism

1. What inclinations, insights, sensitivities, or concerns have I had that indicate I have the gift of evangelism?

2. How has God used this gift through me to affect the lives of other people?

3. Have others said things about me that have helped to confirm that I have this gift? If so, what?

4. In what ways might this gift be further used . . .

   a. in my personal relationships at home, with friends, or at work?

   b. in the church?

   c. in community-oriented ministries for Christ?

5. What problems or pitfalls, if any, have I encountered in using this gift?

Exploring Evangelism from Scripture

1. Write out the portions of Ephesians 4:11-12 and 2 Timothy 4:5 that identify evangelism as a gift.

2. What does Philip's example tell us about the work of an evangelist, as described in Acts 8:5-6, 12, 26-40?

3. Read Mark 1:16-17. In this passage, to whom was the gift of evangelism given? What were the results as Peter (Simon) exercised this gift on the day of Pentecost (Acts 2:37-41)?

4. What happened as Paul and Barnabas preached the good news in Derbe? What needed to happen after this mass conversion? (See Acts 14:21-22.)

FAITH

Definition

The special Spirit-given ability to know with certainty that God wills to do something and is certain to do it, in response to prayer, even when there is no concrete evidence.

Faith as a Spiritual Gift

The person with the spiritual gift of faith has an extraordinary ability to believe and trust the infinite power of God in specific situations. This is a Spirit-given ability to know what God wants to do, coupled with the utter confidence that he will do it. This confidence comes from an inward conviction given by the Holy Spirit. It is not a contrived mental attitude dependent on the strength of one's own belief.

The spiritual gift of faith (1 Corinthians 12:9) must be distinguished from saving faith, the faith on which our redemption rests. Saving faith is the ability to trust in the atoning work of Christ for salvation. It is required for all Christians in order to be saved. The spiritual gift of faith, on the other hand, is exercised by those who already believe. It is possessed by some, but not all, in the Christian community. It relates to Christian life and ministry, not to the securing of eternal life.

The spiritual gift of faith is of great value to the church. Though not much is said about it in Scripture, there are many evidences of its use. Abraham was probably exercising this gift when he responded to Isaac's question about a lamb for sacrifice by saying, "God himself will provide the lamb" (Genesis 22:8). Jesus was using this gift when, with reference to Lazarus, he said to Martha with absolute confidence, "Your brother will rise again" (John 11:23). Peter acted with the gift of faith when he stepped out of a boat and walked on water at Jesus' invitation (Matthew 14:29). Paul exercised this gift in a dangerous situation when he trusted God's word that he would not be harmed, and he consequently continued to preach with boldness (Acts 18:9-11). God also gave him the faith to know that he and those with him would be spared, even though the ship they were sailing on would be wrecked (Acts 27:21-26).

God uses the gift of faith in many ways. He brings glory to himself as those with this gift praise and extol his name in the face of adverse circumstances. The church is encouraged, through those who exercise this gift, to remember that God holds the future in his hand. The gift of faith helps individuals and churches to face crises with confidence and to meet challenges with boldness. Jesus may have been referring to this gift when he spoke of faith that could move mountains (Matthew 21:21-22).

Characteristics of the Person with the Gift of Faith

If this is a working gift for me,

- I have had the experience of knowing with certainty that God willed to do something, and then I saw him do it in response to faith and prayer.

- in specific cases God has given me assurance that he would do what seemed unlikely.

- I am often able to trust God to intervene in supernatural ways in spite of evidence to the contrary.

If this is a waiting gift for me,

- I find myself taking God's promises at face value and applying them to given situations without doubt.

- I have a sense for moments when the "prayer of faith" is needed.

- I find it easy to believe that "mountains" are moved by faith (Matthew 21:21-22).

Ways to Use the Gift of Faith

Personal/informal uses:

- claim God's promise for a family member or friend

- be used to bring healing through "the prayer of faith"

Ministries within the church:

- challenge and/or lead the church to renewal

- help keep up hope in a discouraging situation

Community-oriented ministries for Christ:

- know God's will in developing a new ministry

Potential Liabilities in the Gift of Faith

A person with the gift of faith can sometimes tend to

- pass judgment on those who do not have such faith.

- exercise the gift of faith without love (1 Corinthians 13:2).

- be impatient with those who are quite cautious.

Faith as a Responsibility of All Christians

Some Christians have the spiritual gift of faith, but every Christian must have saving faith to be a Christian. Jesus encourages *all* to believe (John 6:29; 14:1) and makes faith the ground of salvation (John 20:31). Believers are saved by grace through faith (Ephesians 2:8). In addition, all believers are called to trust God in all circumstances of life, believing that he will keep his promises and work things out "for the good of those who love him" (Romans 8:28). Those who trust him fully are blessed and rewarded (Hebrews 11:39-40).

Discerning the Gift of Faith

1. What inner inclinations, insights, sensitivities, or concerns have I had that indicate I have the gift of faith?

2. How has God used this gift through me to affect the lives of other people?

3. Have others said things about me that have helped to confirm that I have this gift? If so, what?

4. In what ways might this gift be further used . . .

   a. in my personal relationships at home, with friends, or at work?

   b. in the church?

   c. in community-oriented ministries for Christ?

5. What problems or pitfalls, if any, have I encountered in using this gift?

Exploring Faith from Scripture

1. See 1 Corinthians 12:8-9. Write out the key phrase identifying faith as a gift of the Spirit.

2. What is the difference between the gift of faith identified in 1 Corinthians 12:9 and the saving faith mentioned in Romans 3:22 and 5:1?

3. Read Romans 4:18-22 and Hebrews 11:11-12. Who exercised this gift? What was the ground of his confidence? The result?

4. What is the power of such faith, according to Matthew 21:18-22?

5. What motive is essential when exercising the gift of faith (see 1 Corinthians 13:2)? What is likely to happen if this motive is absent?

6. What is the value of the gift of faith in the Christian life (Hebrews 11:32-40)? How do you explain the fact that some of these heroes of faith seemed to go down to defeat (11:35-40)?

GIVING

Definition

The special Spirit-given ability to contribute significant personal and material resources to the Lord's work freely, cheerfully, and sacrificially.

Giving as a Spiritual Gift

The spiritual gift of giving is identified in Romans 12:8 along with several other gifts. The Greek word that Paul uses to describe this gift places the emphasis on "giving or sharing of ourselves" as we give. This involves giving that responds to a specific need, giving in which we share not only our resources but also ourselves. The gift of giving celebrates the compassionate concern of the giver.

The gift of giving does not belong exclusively to high-income people. The Macedonian Christians were impoverished, but by the grace of God "their extreme poverty welled up in rich generosity," says Paul, so that they gave "even beyond their ability" (2 Corinthians 8:1-3). The amount that is given is not the issue. Rather, the gift of giving has to do with the attitude and the spirit of the giver. Paul touches on attitude when he reports that the Macedonians gave "out of . . . their overflowing joy" and "urgently pleaded with [Paul] for the privilege of sharing in this service" (2 Corinthians 8:2, 4). Jesus commended the spirit of self-sacrifice of a poor widow who gave all she had (Luke 21:1-3), and he held up that spirit as a model for all. Dorcas, too, is a fine example of a person with a giving attitude: she gave of her own material goods, and she gave freely of her spiritual gifts (creative ability, mercy, service) to help clothe the poor (Acts 9:36-39). In bringing the gospel, the apostles (as well as their many companions) also gave freely of their entire lives—many of them were even executed for their faith.

While certain individuals have the spiritual gift of giving, all believers have the responsibility to give. How do these two differ? The spiritually gifted giver is distinguished by a willing attitude and spirit. The apostle Paul's attitude toward the Thessalonian Christians illustrates this. He said to them, "We loved you so much that we were delighted to share with you not only the gospel of God but our lives as well, because you had become so dear to us" (1 Thessalonians 2:8). This passage uses the same word for "giving" that Romans 12:8 uses in referring to the gift of giving. Gifted givers have a strong interest in the people and the causes they support; they see money and all their resources as a way to serve God.

Characteristics of the Spiritually Gifted Giver

If this is a working gift for me,

- I find great joy in giving, and I look for ways to meet human needs by giving of myself as well as of my material resources.
- I give cheerfully and liberally, often above what is expected.
- I take strong personal interest in the causes and people I support, and I see giving as a way to minister.

If this is a waiting gift for me,

- I am easily moved to give when I become aware of a need or opportunity in people's lives or in God's kingdom.
- I am willing to make personal sacrifices and maintain a lower standard of living in order to benefit God's work.
- I see money and possessions as tools to serve God, and I regularly set them aside for this purpose.

Ways to Use the Gift of Giving

Personal/informal uses:

- assist a person financially
- help a Christian friend discover the joy of giving
- make a strategic, no-interest loan
- practice giving of my time and talents to serve others

Ministries within the church:

- contribute generously to my church from my material goods and my giftedness
- teach a stewardship class
- give liberally to other kingdom causes

Community-oriented ministries for Christ:

- support a benevolent organization with regular gifts
- invest "seed money" in a new cause
- assist in organizing a fund drive

Potential Liabilities in the Gift of Giving

A person with this gift can sometimes tend to

- be proud of giving.
- condemn as unspiritual those who do not give self-sacrificially.
- try to buy influence or position with their gifts.
- be unduly critical of how others spend their money.

Giving as a Responsibility of All Christians

Even if only some believers have the spiritual gift of giving, all believers are challenged to give. Scripture teaches, "Each of you must bring a gift in proportion to the way the LORD your God has blessed you" (Deuteronomy 16:17). And "if you want to give, your gift will be accepted. It will be judged by what you have, not by what you do not have" (2 Corinthians 8:12, NCV). Further, Proverbs 3:9-10 says, "Honor the LORD with your wealth, with the firstfruits of all your crops," and it promises, "Then your barns will be filled to overflowing, and your vats will brim over with new wine." When we give freely of all we have to the Lord, trusting that he will provide all we need, he graciously gives more than we need so that we can keep on giving—for the upbuilding and strengthening of the kingdom (2 Corinthians 9:8-11).

Discerning the Gift of Giving

1. What inclinations, insights, sensitivities, or concerns have I had that indicate I have the gift of giving?

2. How has God used this gift through me to affect the lives of other people?

3. Have others said things about me that have helped to confirm that I have this gift? If so, what?

4. In what ways might this gift be further used . . .

   a. in my personal relationships at home, with friends, or at work?

   b. in the church?

   c. in community-oriented ministries for Christ?

5. What problems or pitfalls, if any, have I encountered in using this gift?

Exploring Giving from Scripture

1. Write out the portion of Romans 12:8 that identifies the spiritual gift of giving. How does Paul say this gift is to be used?

2. Acts 4:32-37 shows how the gift of giving functioned in the early church. Who especially exercised the gift of giving here? What were the results of this giving in the Christian community?

3. What do we learn about the function of giving in Luke 8:1-3?

4. What can we learn from 2 Corinthians 8:1-7 about exercising the gift of giving?

5. According to 2 Corinthians 9:6-15, how are we to give? How is it that we are able to give? What promise does God make to the giver? What's the result in the Christian community?

6. Is it necessary to be wealthy to exercise the gift of giving? (See Luke 21:1-4; 1 Corinthians 16:2.) Explain.

HEALING

Definition

The special Spirit-given ability to serve as an instrument through whom God brings physical, emotional, and spiritual healing in an extraordinary way.

Healing as a Spiritual Gift

Healing is identified as a spiritual gift in 1 Corinthians 12:9: "To another [is given] gifts of healing by that one Spirit." Note that *gifts* is plural, suggesting a variety of abilities relating to various maladies and diseases.

Jesus frequently exercised gifts of healing. The Bible states thirty-eight times that he is involved in individual or multiple healings. In addition, the book of Acts identifies seventeen healings by the apostle Paul and others. James assigns to the elders the task of praying for the sick. They are to offer prayers "in faith [that] will make the sick person well; the Lord will raise him up" (James 5:15). There is no indication that the Lord expected healing ministries of this type to discontinue before his return.

The purpose of healing gifts, as well as other spiritual gifts, is to testify to the gospel (Hebrews 2:4). Mark verifies this when he says that the preached word is confirmed "by the signs that accompanied it" (Mark 16:20). Through gifts of healing, God shows his concern for the body as well as the soul. The ultimate goal of the kingdom of God is wholeness in Christ.

The gifts of healing do not do away with the need for doctors and nurses. God is glorified through healing by medical means as well as by extraordinary means. There are no universally valid means of healing given in Scripture. Faith, prayer, anointing, a word of command, and laying on hands are often but not always mentioned. There is no "magic formula" in healing. The gift of faith, however, seems most important in combination with healing. People with potential for these gifts also have unusual compassion for the sick. Further, guidance of the Spirit in healing is essential. Emotional healing is as much a part of this gift as physical healing is. The gift of healing may be linked to the gift of faith in such a way that the individual knows that God will heal in a specific situation.

Characteristics of the Person with the Gift of Healing

If this is a working gift for me,

- I have faith that God can and does heal apart from the use of natural means.

- I pray expectantly for persons who are physically, emotionally, or spiritually ill.

- people have experienced healing from God as a result of my ministries.

If this is a waiting gift for me,

- I have an unusual amount of compassion for the sick.

- I am drawn to ministries that offer care and healing to hurting persons.

- I am aware that God has given me a healing touch that needs to be more fully developed.

Ways to Use the Gift of Healing

Personal/informal uses:

- pray in faith with persons who are sick, lay on hands, and anoint with oil when so led by the Spirit

- respond to prayer burdens from the Holy Spirit for sick and suffering persons

- position myself for healing ministries by becoming involved in ministries to hurting people

Ministries within the church:

- join an intercession team

- become involved in a Stephen Ministry

- accompany pastors or church shepherds as they make pastoral visits

- be the designated intercessor in a need-based support group organized to help people cope with a physical, emotional, or spiritual problem

- participate in a deliverance ministry

Community-oriented ministries for Christ:

- work alongside doctors praying for the well-being of persons who are diseased

- offer my services to agencies who give counseling to emotionally disturbed persons

- serve as a hospital volunteer at a medical or psychiatric hospital

- become involved with a national cancer society, AIDS organization, or other agency offering care services to my community

Potential Liabilities in the Gift of Healing

A person with this gift can sometimes tend to

- try to heal anyone at any time, without an appropriate discerning of the Spirit's guidance.

- become rigid about using certain methods that are not confirmed in Scripture.

- make healing dependent on the sick person's faith.

- identify the power of healing with the human agent instead of with Christ.

- become impatient when healing doesn't happen.

Healing as a Responsibility of All Christians

Every Christian can be used of God to heal. Various persons are used in different ways with different people. Sometimes God works through healing teams. Emotional healing may come through those who are able to listen in a loving and sympathetic way. Spiritual healing may happen through those who exhort and encourage. Demons may be driven out through fervent prayer and truth encounters. Because the healing Spirit resides in all believers, he can use us all.

Discerning the Gift of Healing

1. What inclinations, insights, sensitivities, or concerns have I had that indicate I have gifts of healing?

2. How has God used this gift through me to affect the lives of other people?

3. Have others said things about me that have helped to confirm that I have this gift? If so, what?

4. What are some ways I could use this gift . . .

   a. in my personal relationships at home? with friends? at work?

   b. in the church?

   c. in community-oriented ministries for Christ?

5. What problems or pitfalls, if any, have I encountered in using this gift?

Exploring Healing from Scripture

1. Write out the phrases from 1 Corinthians 12:9, 28 that identify gifts of healing. Why do you suppose the words "gifts" is plural?

2. What do Exodus 15:26; 23:25, and Psalm 103:3 teach us about God and healing?

3. Read Matthew 9:35 and Mark 6:56. How integral would you judge healing was to Jesus' ministry? What do 1 John 3:8 and Acts 10:38 teach us about Jesus' healing ministry? What is the purpose of healing, according to Hebrews 2:4?

4. Who was responsible for Paul's physical afflictions described in 2 Corinthians 12:7-10? Why did God not heal him and remove the affliction? What does this teach us about God's readiness to heal? Should any person with enough faith expect to be healed?

5. What do 2 Kings 20:1-7 and 1 Timothy 5:23 tell us about God's use of ordinary and extraordinary means to heal?

6. What can we learn from John 14:11-14 about Jesus' expectations regarding gifts of healing?

HOSPITALITY

Definition

The special Spirit-given ability to love, welcome, and graciously serve guests and strangers so that they feel at home.

Hospitality as a Spiritual Gift

Hospitality is not expressly mentioned as a gift in Scripture. However, the apostle Peter refers to it in such a way as to suggest that it's one of the gifts conferred on the church by the Spirit for building up the body and for community ministry (1 Peter 4:9-10).

The word *hospitable* literally means "given to love of strangers." The hospitable person is one who is comfortable entertaining not only friends or relatives but also strangers. Hospitable people are able to make others feel at home in their presence, in their home, or in their church. The comfort of the guest or stranger is a priority higher than their own comfort. Those with this gift truly love hosting others.

God himself demonstrated hospitality by loving strangers from all nations. "These [strangers] I will bring to my holy mountain and give them joy in my house of prayer," he says (Isaiah 56:7). Jesus exercised this gift when he welcomed sinners and ate with them (Luke 15:1-2), and he challenged his followers to "invite the poor, the crippled, the lame, [and] the blind" instead of focusing exclusively on friends and relatives (Luke 14:12-14). Lydia exemplified this gift by showing hospitality to Paul and his companions (Acts 16:15).

Readiness to provide board and lodging for friends and travelers was particularly important in the first century, which lacked a system of guest facilities for ordinary people. Elders and widows in particular were expected to show hospitality (1 Timothy 3:2; 5:10). Diotrephes was reprimanded for failing to show hospitality (3 John 9-10). Gaius, however, was commended for his hospitality to strangers (3 John 5-8)—a hospitality enjoyed by Paul and the church he had planted (Romans 16:23).

Characteristics of the Person with the Gift of Hospitality

If this is a working gift for me,

- I enjoy providing a haven for guests, and I do not feel imposed upon by unexpected visitors.
- I have a knack for making strangers feel at ease in my home and at church.
- my home is always open to those in need of hospitality.

If this is a waiting gift for me,

- I am sensitive to offer small acts of kindness that make a difference for guests or strangers.
- I tend to be more aware of the needs of guests than of my own needs.
- I have a genuine appreciation for each person to whom I show hospitality.

Ways to Use the Gift of Hospitality

Personal/informal uses:

- display gracious openness to strangers
- entertain in my home
- welcome students, military service workers, and others who are temporarily away from home into my family circle

Ministries within the church:

- be a greeter or usher
- make welcome calls to those who have visited the church
- help new members get assimilated
- host the church's coffee hour

Community-oriented ministries for Christ:

- be a receptionist at a nursing home
- befriend foreign students
- become involved in refugee resettlement

Potential Liabilities in the Gift of Hospitality

A person with this gift can sometimes tend to

- allow people to take undue advantage of his or her hospitality.
- come on too strong and overwhelm reticent people.
- not be able to say no when he or she really should.

Hospitality as a Responsibility of All Christians

The Bible encourages all Christians to be hospitable. God told his people in the Old Testament, "Treat [foreigners] just as you treat your own citizens. Love foreigners as you love yourselves, because you were foreigners one time in Egypt" (Leviticus 19:33-34). Paul includes the command "practice hospitality" in his list of Christian duties in Romans 12:9-21. And Hebrews 13:2 states, "Do not forget to entertain strangers."

Discerning the Gift of Hospitality

1. What inclinations, insights, sensitivities, or concerns have I had that indicate I have the gift of hospitality?

2. How has God used this gift through me to affect the lives of other people?

3. Have others said things about me that have helped to confirm that I have this gift? If so, what?

4. In what ways could this gift be further used . . .

   a. in my personal relationships at home, with friends, or at work?

   b. in the church?

   c. in community-oriented ministries for Christ?

5. What problems or pitfalls, if any, have I encountered in using this gift?

Exploring Hospitality from Scripture

1. With what attitude should hospitality be offered, according to 1 Peter 4:9?

2. Read Hebrews 13:1-2. Why is the practice of hospitality important?

3. Who especially are called to be hospitable, according to 1 Timothy 3:2 and Titus 1:7-8? Why?

4. How did hospitality operate in the lives of active widows? See 1 Timothy 5:9-10.

5. Read Acts 16:14-15. How did Lydia exemplify the gift of hospitality?

INTERCESSION

Definition

The special Spirit-given ability to pray faithfully and effectively for others for extended periods and to see many specific answers to those prayers.

Intercession as a Spiritual Gift

Intercession is not expressly identified as a spiritual gift in the New Testament. There are scriptural examples, however, of extraordinary ministries of intercession. Our Lord's example in prayer stands out above all. The gospels record eighteen references to Jesus' prayer life, eight prayers that he prayed, and fourteen different prayer themes about which he taught. Two passages speak of his ongoing high-priestly ministry of prayer from heaven (Romans 8:34; Hebrews 7:25). Paul's record of interceding on behalf of the churches he established is also truly remarkable. On ten occasions in his letters to the churches he reports the content of his intercessory prayers for them (for example, see 1 Thessalonians 1:2-3).

In the Old Testament Abraham stands out as an intercessor in his earnest prayer for Sodom (Genesis 18:22-33). Moses interceded faithfully and effectively for idolatrous Israel (Exodus 32:31-32; Psalm 106:23). Samuel, too, interceded constantly for God's people with an awareness that to fail to pray was to sin: "As for me," he said, "far be it from me that I should sin against the LORD by failing to pray for you" (1 Samuel 12:23). Elijah was also an example of a righteous person whose prayers were "powerful and effective" (James 5:16-18; see 1 Kings 17:21-22; 18:42-45).

The Old Testament (Hebrew) word for "intercession" means "to assail God with requests." And the New Testament (Greek) word for this kind of prayer has in it the idea of "a heart concern for others in which one stands between them and God making request on their behalf" (*Baker Dictionary of Theology*). Intercession is, however, more than verbal requests. It involves a way of life, for one cannot intercede without a willingness to be involved. The one who stands between God and someone else represents both; pleading the person's cause to God and representing God's concern to the person.

Characteristics of the Spiritually Gifted Intercessor

If this is a working gift for me,

- I consider the prayer requests of others seriously, and I faithfully pray for them for extended periods.
- I pay a price when I pray, agonizing over and identifying with those for whom I pray.

- I am conscious of ministering to others as I pray for them, releasing God's power and grace in their lives.

If this is a waiting gift for me,

- I am alert to the prayer needs of others, and I am concerned to give them needed prayer support.
- I am motivated to pray by an inner conviction that God does things in response to prayer that he wouldn't do otherwise.
- I would like to advance the Lord's work through interceding regularly for believers in ministry.

Ways to Use the Gift of Intercession

Personal/informal uses:

- faithfully intercede for friends, family, and others
- pray with persons who have special needs
- lead a prayer group at my workplace

Ministries within the church:

- be a prayer partner to believers in a specific ministry
- lead a prayer cell
- help develop a prayer ministry

Community-oriented ministries for Christ:

- pray for local and national governments
- become a prayer partner to a parachurch agency
- start a neighborhood prayer ministry

Potential Liabilities in the Gift of Intercession

A person with this gift can sometimes tend to

- become mechanical in the use of prayer lists.
- take pride in much praying.
- assume that prayer is a substitute for action.

Intercession as a Responsibility of All Christians

Every Christian is called to pray for others. "Pray for each other," writes James; "when a believing person prays, great things happen" (James 5:16, NCV). "Devote yourselves to prayer, being watchful and thankful," Paul charged the Colossians (Colossians 4:2). Prayer is required of all believers so that all may stand against the devil's schemes. After admonishing believers to put on the whole armor of God, Paul concludes, "Pray in the Spirit on all occasions with all kinds of prayers and requests. With this in mind, be alert and always keep on praying for all the saints" (Ephesians 6:18).

Discerning the Gift of Intercession

1. What inclinations, insights, sensitivities, or concerns have I had that indicate I have the gift of intercession?

2. How has God used this gift through me to affect the lives of other people?

3. Have others said things about me that have helped to confirm that I have this gift? If so, what?

4. In what ways could this gift be further used . . .

   a. in my personal relationships at home, with friends, or at work?

   b. in the church?

   c. in community-oriented ministries for Christ?

5. What problems or pitfalls, if any, have I encountered in using this gift?

Exploring Intercession from Scripture

1. What was the tenor of Paul's prayers for members of the churches he had planted (Ephesians 1:16-19; Philippians 1:3-6; Colossians 1:9-12)? What difference do you suppose it made in the lives of the believers in those churches as God answered Paul's prayers?

2. What place did strong intercessory prayer have in the church, according to James 5:14-16?

3. What are some of the results of intercessory prayer, according to . . .

   a. Ephesians 6:18-20?

   b. 1 Timothy 2:1-4?

   c. James 5:16b-18?

4. What is the Holy Spirit's role in the prayers of believers? (See Romans 8:26-27.)

5. What difference did prayer make in the battle that Israel fought against the Amalekites (Exodus 17:8-18)? Who deserved the credit for this victory?

INTERPRETATION OF TONGUES

Definition

The special Spirit-given ability to interpret into known language a message spoken in tongues.

Interpretation of Tongues as a Spiritual Gift

There are two types of tongues—private and public. The private tongue-speaker praises God in an unknown language and is personally edified (1 Corinthians 14:4). No interpretation is required. Public tongue-speaking, however, requires interpretation. The interpretation may be supplied by the tongue-speaking person (14:5, 13) or by another person (14:27). The tongue-speaking, once interpreted, edifies not only the tongue-speaker but also all who are present. If there is no one to interpret, the tongue-speaker "should keep quiet in the church and speak to himself and God" (14:28).

Those who have experienced tongues and interpretation of tongues say that the interpretation is usually not a word-for-word translation but instead gives the sense of the message.

Tongues, once interpreted, are basically equivalent to prophecy. The guidelines that apply to prophecy also apply to the interpretations of tongues. (See the gift study on prophecy in this section of the manual.)

Characteristics of the Person with the Gift of Interpretation of Tongues

If this is a working gift for me,

- I get an idea about what God is saying when I hear someone speak in tongues.

- believers gathered in public worship have been edified by interpretations I have given of tongues.

- I have spoken in tongues and have also received an interpretation of them.

If this is a waiting gift for me,

- I am drawn to worship services where tongues are expected, and I have a heightened sense that God is speaking to us through tongues.

- an interpretation I received from the Spirit was confirmed when someone more experienced in tongue-interpretation gave publicly the very interpretation I had received.

- I am sensitive to impressions of the Holy Spirit.

Ways to Use the Gift of Interpretation of Tongues

Personal/informal uses:

- receive an interpretation from the Holy Spirit when privately speaking in tongues

Ministries within the church:

- interpret tongues spoken in public worship

- interpret tongues spoken in a small group so that everyone in the group may be edified

- instruct and coach others who have the potential for the gift of interpretation of tongues

Community-oriented ministries for Christ:

- report to the community any interpretation that is meant for them

Potential Liabilities of the Gift of Interpretation of Tongues

A person with this gift can sometimes tend to

- give a word that did not come from the Holy Spirit.

- take personal glory in the manifestation of the gift.

- count himself or herself as superior to others who do not have this gift.

Interpretation of Tongues as a Responsibility of All Christians

The key issue in interpretation of tongues is receiving a message directly from God that will edify oneself and others. Though most Christians will not likely possess this gift, all should be as open as possible to impressions the Holy Spirit may desire to give in order to build us up. Jesus said, "My sheep listen to my voice" (John 10:27). Jesus regularly heard and responded to the voice of the Father.

Discerning the Gift of Interpretation of Tongues

1. What inclinations, insights, sensitivities, or concerns have I had that indicate I have the gift of interpreting tongues?

2. How has God used this gift through me to affect the lives of other people?

3. Have others said things about me that have helped to confirm that I have this gift? If so, what?

4. In what ways could this gift be further used . . .

   a. in my personal relationships at home, with friends, or at work?

   b. in the church?

   c. in community-oriented ministries for Christ?

5. What problems or pitfalls, if any, have I encountered in using this gift?

Exploring Interpretation of Tongues from Scripture

1. Write out the phrases from 1 Corinthians 12:10, 30 that confirm the gift of interpreting tongues in Scripture.

2. What purpose is served by interpretation of tongues, according to 1 Corinthians 14:5, 12-13, 26?

3. What guidelines relate to the use of tongues and interpretation of tongues in public worship, according to 1 Corinthians 14:13, 27-28?

KNOWLEDGE

Definition

The special Spirit-given ability to receive from God knowledge that is crucial to ministry and that could not have been obtained in other ways.

Knowledge as a Spiritual Gift

In Greek the word for "message of knowledge" in 1 Corinthians 12:8 is literally "a deep knowing." The New Testament does not make clear whether this means learned knowledge or revealed knowledge. Interpreters go both ways. Peter Wagner defines this gift as "the ability . . . to discover, accumulate, analyze, and clarify information and ideas" (*Your Spiritual Gifts Can Help Your Church Grow*). Bob Whitaker, however, says this gift "is not about intellectual ability or learning; it is an inner knowing or intuition such as was seen in Jesus' ministry when he knew what his critics were thinking, feeling or plotting, and then spoke in response as though he had read their minds" (*In the Spirit's Power;* see Mark 2:8; Luke 6:8; 7:36-47; 9:47).

While no one can say for certain exactly what Paul had in mind in 1 Corinthians 12:8, there are reasons to believe that he was talking about knowledge or information received directly from the Lord. First, such a meaning fits best into this context where all of the other gifts mentioned have a strong supernatural dimension. Second, it is doubtful that, at this early stage of church history, before the completion of the canon and the availability of personal Bibles, intellectual learning would have developed sufficiently for Paul to have mentioned it. Third, and most important, often in the Old Testament and at least fifteen times in Jesus' ministry and seven times in Acts we observe just such a reception of knowledge directly from God. In other words, we observe the gift in use. In each case the knowledge was crucial to ministry. So while the Greek word for "knowledge" in 1 Corinthians 12:8 is imprecise, the Scriptures help us arrive at a suitable definition.

The knowledge that this gift brings is not on the same plane as the special revelation of the Bible. Nor is it intended to add to what Scripture teaches. It is essentially guidance: knowledge or information given by the Holy Spirit that relates to a specific situation or moment. It is not valid beyond its own time and place. Its validity relates to a context in which the Spirit desires to guide or minister for the glory of God. This localized "message of knowledge" is always subject to the truth of the Scriptures and will never contradict it.

The communication revealed in the gift of knowledge may come in various forms, such as feelings, words, nudges, images, insights, thoughts, impressions, or a word of Scripture that will intrude into one's thoughts. The gift is supernatural in that the information received could not have been obtained in any way other than directly from God, who knows all things.

Characteristics of the Person with the Gift of Knowledge

If this is a working gift for me,

- I know the difference between my own thoughts and information I have received from the Lord.
- God has revealed to me knowledge of things that would happen before they actually came to pass.
- I sometimes experience God-given, supernatural insights when I am praying.

If this is a waiting gift for me,

- I regularly receive impressions from the Lord through his Holy Spirit.
- when talking with a troubled person, I sometimes discern the previously undetected root hurt without being told.
- I sometimes know things without knowing how I came to know them.

Ways to Use the Gift of Knowledge

Personal/informal uses:

- use God-given information to help a person whom the Lord has brought into my life
- help others avoid danger by means of knowledge I have received
- counsel others who are making long-term decisions

Ministries within the church:

- preach or teach with greater effectiveness because the Lord has supernaturally given me awareness of need and issues
- be part of a healing ministry team with Christians having other strategic gifts
- be involved in a counseling ministry where I am often able to discern the root hurts and speak a word of comfort or encouragement

Community-oriented ministries for Christ:

- serve as a volunteer with a counseling agency
- work with an evangelistic team

Potential Liabilities in the Gift of Knowledge

A person with this gift can sometimes tend to

- become puffed up because of insights discerned and messages revealed.

- communicate publicly a word of knowledge that was meant to be private.

- fake the word of knowledge when no revelation has come.

Knowledge as a Responsibility of All Christians

It is necessary for every believer to have knowledge of God's revelation. For those not given knowledge as a spiritual gift, the knowledge of God's revelation will come primarily through study of the Word of God and through those who preach and teach. Often when a person is reading or hearing God's Word, the Spirit will impress a particular truth upon the individual or give heightened insight and understanding of the Scriptures. Careful and diligent study of the Word of God will help every believer grow spiritually and be effective in ministry.

Discerning the Gift of Knowledge

1. What inclinations, insights, sensitivities, or concerns have I had that indicate I have the gift of knowledge?

2. How has God used this gift through me to affect the lives of other people?

3. Have others said things about me that have helped to confirm that I have this gift? If so, what?

4. In what ways could this gift be further used . . .

    a. in my personal relationships at home, with friends, or at work?

    b. in the church?

    c. in community-oriented ministries for Christ?

5. What problems or pitfalls, if any, have I encountered in using this gift?

Exploring Knowledge from Scripture

1. Write out the phrase from 1 Corinthians 12:8 that identifies the gift of knowledge.

2. How did a word of knowledge revealed in John 4:17-18 help Jesus to minister effectively to a Samaritan woman?

3. What do we see in Acts 5:1-11 to indicate that Peter had the gift of knowledge?

4. What is the message of knowledge referred to in Ephesians 3:1-6? How significant was this for Paul's ministry?

5. Read Matthew 16:13-18. What word of knowledge did Peter receive?

LEADERSHIP

Definition

The special Spirit-given ability to lead others by seeing and casting a vision, setting and communicating goals, and inspiring and directing people to work together toward those goals.

Leadership as a Spiritual Gift

Leadership is listed by Paul as a spiritual gift in Romans 12:8. The Greek word used there identifies a person who "stands before," rules, leads, or directs. The help given by the leader is often for the well-being of the person led. The leader cares for or gives aid. Moreover, the tense of the verb in Romans 12:8 suggests that the leader also participates in the activity being led. He or she is a kind of "player-coach," according to various Bible scholars.

Romans 12:8 states that the one who leads must do so "diligently." Diligence involves doing one's best, exerting oneself, putting forth an intense effort. Paul's diligence in leading is evident in 2 Thessalonians 3:7-9: "We were not idle when we were with you, nor did we eat anyone's food without paying for it. On the contrary, we worked night and day, laboring and toiling so that we would not be a burden to any of you."

Nehemiah is a good example of a spiritually gifted leader who exercised his gift. He cast a vision for rebuilding the walls of Jerusalem, established and communicated goals to accomplish the task, and inspired and directed those who followed him to work together toward a common purpose. He was concerned about the welfare of the people living in a city without walls, so he gained the confidence of those who were needed to do the work, and he provided direction to bring the whole project to a glorious conclusion (see Nehemiah 2:11-20; 4:14; 12:27-43). Nehemiah was also a gifted administrator (see Nehemiah 4:11-13, 16-23). (See the gift study on administration for a comparison of leadership and administration as different yet related gifts.)

The Bible gives direction to church leaders in their leadership roles. Those who are chosen to lead or rule must demonstrate their ability first in their own homes (1 Timothy 3:4). Elders are to "direct the affairs of the church" (1 Timothy 5:17) and serve "as overseers—not because [they] must, but because [they] are willing, as God wants [them] to be; not greedy for money, but eager to serve; not lording it over those entrusted to [them], but being examples to the flock" (1 Peter 5:2-3). The Scriptures also speak to those who are led: "Respect those who work hard among you, who are over you in the Lord and who admonish you. Hold them in the highest regard in love because of their work" (1 Thessalonians 5:12-13).

Characteristics of the Spiritually Gifted Leader

If this is a working gift for me,

- I have provided the overall vision for a task and given direction for its completion.
- I have been used of God to motivate others who willingly followed and worked together in a kingdom project.
- I have served effectively as a leader by setting clear goals and involving people in working toward those goals.

If this is a waiting gift for me,

- I am able to present the vision for a task in a manner that attracts others to get involved.
- I have a sense for motivating and directing others in a project.
- I am quick to sense when a group I am part of is spinning its wheels for lack of leadership, and I sense the need to take charge.

Ways to Use the Gift of Leadership

Personal/informal uses:

- manage my own life well
- lead my family in a project
- help a friend set long-term objectives

Ministries within the church:

- chair a committee
- spearhead a new movement
- help the church establish long-range plans

Community-oriented ministries for Christ:

- give leadership in a service agency
- serve on a steering committee for a new retirement home
- serve in political office

Potential Liabilities in the Gift of Leadership

The spiritually gifted leader can sometimes tend to

- be insensitive to those involved in carrying out details of the vision.
- get too far ahead of his or her followers.
- take pride in position or power.
- make projects more important than people.
- be more authority-conscious than ministry-conscious.

Leadership as a Responsibility of All Christians

The leader is a person who is usually a step or two ahead, who sets goals for the future, and who motivates people toward those goals. Every Christian has these responsibilities in one way or another. Parents lead their children. Mature Christians lead new Christians. Elders and deacons lead in the church. All Christians should look ahead and set goals for their own spiritual development. The importance of planning for the future was surely in Jesus' mind when he spoke of counting the cost before building a tower (Luke 14:28-30). Paul was concerned to make goal-oriented planning a part of every Christian's life when he spoke of pressing on toward the goal "to win the prize for which God has called us heavenward in Christ Jesus" (Philippians 3:14). In this sense, all Christians have leadership responsibility.

Discerning the Gift of Leadership

1. What inclinations, insights, sensitivities, or concerns have I had that indicate I have the gift of leadership?

2. How has God used this gift through me to affect the lives of other people?

3. Have others said things about me that have helped to confirm that I have this gift? If so, what have they said?

4. In what ways could this gift be further used . . .

   a. in my personal relationships at home, with friends, or at work?

   b. in the church?

   c. in community-oriented ministries for Christ?

5. What problems or pitfalls, if any, have I encountered in using this gift?

Exploring Leadership from Scripture

1. Write out the part of Romans 12:8 where Paul identifies leadership as a gift. Note that some translations use "give aid " or "have authority" instead of "lead."

2. What was the role of church leaders as noted in Hebrews 13:7? How were followers to benefit from their leaders?

3. What qualifications for leadership are apparent in David (Psalm 78:72)?

4. What does 1 Thessalonians 5:12-13 reveal to us about leadership in the church? What is expected of followers?

5. Describe in your own words the attitude required of a leader as shown by Jesus in Luke 22:24-27.

6. What characteristics of a good leader are apparent from 2 Thessalonians 3:7-10?

MERCY

Definition

The special Spirit-given ability to feel genuine empathy and compassion for hurting people and to translate that feeling into cheerful acts of service.

Mercy as a Spiritual Gift

People with the spiritual gift of mercy cheerfully and effectively show Christ's love and compassion as they reach out to all who suffer. Dr. Daniel Fuller defines mercy as "compassion so great that it stoops to aid even the most pitiable and undeserving." The gift involves a deep and extraordinary compassion that transcends normal human caring. Cheerfulness should be the attitude with which mercy is shown.

The recipients of the gift of mercy are the sick, the aged, the physically or mentally challenged or disabled, the homebound, the poor, the homeless, the imprisoned—any who are in troubled situations. Mercy is also to be extended to those who are spiritually unhealthy and in bondage to Satan. In fact, our acts of mercy may be our best witness to those outside the kingdom (Matthew 25:35-45).

The person with this gift not only feels deeply but is moved to action. Jesus demonstrated the action of mercy in his frequent reaching out to the sick, the suffering, and the outcasts of his society. The good Samaritan in Jesus' story showed compassion toward a helpless victim and paid the price of involvement at great risk and cost to himself (Luke 10:30-37). Dorcas, a devoted follower of Christ, combined feeling and action in her use of the gift of mercy. She was "always doing good and helping the poor" (Acts 9:36). James points out that mercy should be not simply caring but also sharing: "Suppose a brother or sister is without clothes and daily food. If one of you says to him, 'Go, I wish you well; keep warm and well fed,' but does nothing about his physical needs, what good is it?" (James 2:15-16).

Characteristics of the Person with the Gift of Mercy

If this is a working gift for me,

- I feel deeply for hurting people and have a gift for turning compassion into practical help, cheerfully done.

- I enjoy ministering to those who suffer physical, mental, or emotional troubles, and I do it regularly.

- with the Spirit's help, I am effective in ministering to hurting people who often attest to the blessing they have received.

If this is a waiting gift for me,

- I am drawn to those who hurt, and I am eager to give them aid.

- the sight of misery always makes me want to find a way to express God's love to those who suffer.

- kindness and compassion are so much a lifestyle for me that needy persons are attracted to me.

Ways to Use the Gift of Mercy

Personal/informal uses:

- help a sick neighbor

- send cards to persons with special needs

- be a good listener

Ministries within the church:

- make calls to persons who are homebound

- stock an emergency food pantry

- learn how to sign for people who are deaf

- be an advocate for people who are disabled

Community-oriented ministries for Christ:

- volunteer to work at a psychiatric hospital

- be a nursing-home helper

- become a foster parent to physically challenged adults

- be involved in a pregnancy-crisis center

Potential Liabilities in the Gift of Mercy

A person with this gift can sometimes tend to

- be so sympathetic as to never censor or reprimand.

- be guided by feelings rather than Scripture.

- see only good motives in others.

- respond emotionally without looking at the facts.

- be overly protective of the people cared for.

Mercy as a Responsibility of All Christians

Many Bible passages emphasize mercy as a duty for all Christians. In the Old Testament the prophet Micah announced this as God's intent: "He has showed you . . . what is good. And what does the Lord require of you? To act justly and to love mercy and to walk humbly with your God" (Micah 6:8). In the Sermon on the Mount, Jesus said, "Blessed are the merciful, for they will be shown mercy" (Matthew 5:7), and, "Be merciful, just as your Father is merciful" (Luke 6:36). In his parable of the good Samaritan, Jesus shows that mercy involves a readiness to help the hurting person (Luke 10:30-37). This readiness is required of all believers.

Discerning the Gift of Mercy

1. What inclinations, insights, sensitivities, or concerns have I had that indicate I have the gift of mercy?

2. How has God used this gift through me to affect the lives of other people?

3. Have others said things about me that have helped to confirm that I have this gift? If so, what?

4. In what ways could this gift be further used . . .

   a. in my personal relationships at home, with friends, or at work?

   b. in the church?

   c. in community-oriented ministries for Christ?

5. What problems or pitfalls, if any, have I encountered in using this gift?

Exploring Mercy from Scripture

1. Read Romans 12:8 and write out the phrase that identifies the gift of mercy. With what attitude must the gift be exercised?

2. Look through Luke 4-8 for examples in which Jesus showed mercy. List those examples here.

3. What do we learn from Acts 9:36 about exercising the gift of mercy?

4. What insights can we glean from Luke 6:36 and James 2:15-16 about showing mercy?

5. Read Matthew 25:35-45. To whom is the merciful person really ministering when doing deeds of mercy? What difference does that make?

MIRACLES

Definition

The special Spirit-given ability to serve as an instrument through whom God performs extraordinary works as an expression of his presence and power.

Miracles as a Spiritual Gift

The gift of miracles is identified as a spiritual gift in 1 Corinthians 12:10, which speaks of "miraculous powers." "Workers of miracles" is mentioned in 12:28. Much of the teaching about healing can also be applied to miracles. Many of the astonishing healings of Jesus were miracles. However, the two can be distinguished from each other. The gift of healing primarily addresses illnesses or maladies; the gift of miracles deals more with laws of nature.

Writing in *I Believe in the Holy Spirit*, Michael Green suggests that the miracles Paul had in mind were primarily focused on casting out demons. John Calvin agrees, adding that God "in his severity uses miracles for the destruction of Satan" *(Calvin's New Testament Commentaries*, The First Epistle to the Corinthians). Paul's imposition of blindness upon the magician Elymas (Acts 13:11) and the deaths of Ananias and Sapphira (Acts 5:11) are evidences of God's miraculous severity.

Jesus regularly used the gift of miracles in his ministry. His miracle-working powers were gift powers from God and not simply an exercise of his divinity. Jesus made clear that his power to cast out demons was by the Spirit of God (Matthew 12:28). Among his miracles were turning water into wine (John 2:1-10), calming the wind and sea (Mark 4:35-41), walking on water (Matthew 14:22-32), feeding the five thousand (Matthew 14:13-21), and raising persons from the dead (Mark 5:21-43; Luke 7:11-17; John 11:1-44). The disciples also worked miracles after Jesus' departure, using this spiritual gift in Jesus' name (Acts 3:1-10).

The purposes for miracles are many. Jesus worked miracles to attest to his claims as the Messiah (Acts 2:22). After Jesus' departure, "signs, wonders, and miracles" were "the things that mark[ed] an apostle" (2 Corinthians 12:12). Christ promised to enable believers to do great things in response to their asking so that the Son might "bring glory to the Father" (John 14:12-14). The author to the Hebrews reminds us that it was "by signs, wonders and various miracles, and gifts of the Holy Spirit" that God testified to the gospel (Hebrews 2:3-4).

Many Western Christians have difficulty believing that miracles are part of God's plan today and that they still occur. Our Western worldview tends to exclude this possibility. Christians today should cultivate an awareness to God's miraculous ways of working by meditating on his miracles of the past, by looking for miracles around them, by praying for miracles to take place, and by stepping out in faith and obedience to do God's impossible work.

Characteristics of the Person with the Gift of Miracles

If this is a working gift for me,

- I am confident that God can and does work miracles today, because I have seen them.

- God has used me to demonstrate his miraculous power in a situation where ordinary means were not sufficient.

- I was God's instrument in successfully opposing the devil through God's mighty power.

If this is a waiting gift for me,

- I have a sense for moments when a miraculous display of power would wonderfully glorify God.

- I get excited that God is "able to do immeasurably more than all we ask or imagine" (Ephesians 3:20), and I believe that he wants to demonstrate his power through me.

- when I assess a situation of need or concern, I tend to imagine God's working a powerful miracle to solve the problem.

Ways to Use the Gift of Miracles

Personal/informal uses:

- exorcise demons

- in a desperate situation where there is no possible human solution, ask God for a miracle

Ministries within the church:

- be involved with a deliverance team

- teach others about the spiritual gift of miracles

- stand ready to assist church leaders who face impossible situations

Community-oriented ministries for Christ:

- lead the church to contest spiritual strongholds that grip the community

- through God's power, challenge evil where I see it entrenched in society

Potential Liabilities in the Gift of Miracles

A person with this gift can sometimes tend to

- try to work a miracle without having been guided by the Spirit of the Lord.

- attempt miracles in one's own power.

- take personal credit for what really belongs to the Lord.

Working Miracles as a Responsibility of All Christians

Since the power displayed in a miracle is not the power of humans but that of the sovereign God, he may choose to use any Christian to work a miracle. All believers should remain open to this possibility and trust that the almighty God can use any humble, believing, obedient Christian in this way. Lack of openness and lack of faith can thwart God's desire to use us or bless us through miracles (Matthew 13:58).

Discerning the Gift of Miracles

1. What inclinations, insights, sensitivities, or concerns have I had that indicate I have the gift of miracles?

2. How has God used this gift through me to affect the lives of other people?

3. Have others said things about me that have helped to confirm that I have this gift? If so, what?

4. In what ways could this gift be further used . . .

   a. in my personal relationships at home, with friends, or at work?

   b. in the church?

   c. in community-oriented ministries for Christ?

5. What problems or pitfalls, if any, have I encountered in using this gift?

Exploring Miracles from Scripture

1. Write out the portions of 1 Corinthians 12:10, 28 that mention the spiritual gift of miracles.

2. Miracles are among the mighty works of God in the Old Testament. The plagues upon Egypt (Exodus 7-12), crossing the Red Sea (Exodus 14:21-22), the collapse of Jericho's walls (Joshua 6:1-21), the fiery furnace (Daniel 3), and Jonah's being swallowed by a great fish (Jonah 1:17) are but a few examples. According to Psalm 145:3-7, what is the purpose of such mighty works?

3. In what different ways did miracles serve to advance the kingdom, according to the following verses?

John 3:2; 9:16; 20:30-31

Mark 8:1-10

Acts 5:1-11

Acts 12:1-11; 28:3-6

Acts 13:6-12; Hebrews 2:4

4. Read John 14:12-14. Who is able to do the mighty works of God? How? When? Why?

PROPHECY

Definition

The special Spirit-given ability to receive and communicate a message from God so that believers may be edified and encouraged and so that unbelievers may be convinced.

Prophecy as a Spiritual Gift

The Greek word for "prophecy" means "to speak forth." The word *prophet* in both Hebrew and Greek is defined as "one who speaks for another." Prophecy is the message spoken by the prophet. God, the source of the message, conveys his thoughts to the prophet. Through the prophet God speaks to his people. Before the Scriptures were completed, prophets often received direct revelation. Today the Bible is the prime source of prophetic message—although, of course, the Spirit is free to give guidance as he did through the prophets of biblical times (see Acts 11:28). When the Holy Spirit does speak directly to an immediate situation today, Scripture must be the authority by which the message is judged.

The gift of prophecy is mentioned in every one of the major gift passages in Scripture. Paul considers it a most valuable gift that should be eagerly desired by believers (1 Corinthians 14:1). When prophets speak, hearers must be careful not to "put out the Spirit's fire" and not to "treat prophecies with contempt" (1 Thessalonians 5:19-20). By means of this gift, believers are built up and encouraged, and by it the church is edified (1 Corinthians 14:3-5). Prophecy was a foundational gift for the New Testament church, which is "built on the foundation of the apostles and prophets, with Christ Jesus himself as the chief cornerstone" (Ephesians 2:19-20), and it is one of the gifts God uses to equip believers for ministry (4:11-13). The prediction of future events, though always a possibility by means of the prophetic gift, was never the main focus of the prophet's work. So, too, the focus of prophecy today is upon Christ, who is the Prophet, the Word of God himself (John 1:1, 14). And the place of prophecy is Christ's body, the church.

A sermon may be a vehicle for prophecy, but not all preaching is prophecy. "For preaching to be prophetic, it must stand the test of fidelity to Scripture and compelling application to and insight into the contemporary needs of the people of God" (*Acts of Synod 1973,* p. 452; see also Acts 15:32). Prophecy is God's word to us to apply to our living today, to God's glory.

The words of prophecy must always be tested, for prophets can err. Bob Whitaker, writing in *In the Spirit's Power,* says, "[Prophecy] is a reporting in human words what God has put on our minds. It is a mix of God and human; it is more or less pure and powerful depending upon God's initiative and the receptivity, motives, and spiritual maturity of the speaker. Prophecy, like sermons, can be poor, good, or excellent. That is why it needs to be weighed." In 1 Corinthians 14:29-33, Paul details a plan to weigh what prophets speak. John advises us to "test the spirits to see whether they are from God, because many false prophets have gone out into the world" (1 John 4:1; see also vv. 2-3). Jesus himself similarly warns against false prophets (Matthew 7:15-16).

Characteristics of the Spiritually Gifted Prophet

If this is a working gift for me,

- with a message from God I have pleaded the cause of God to the people of God.

- God is using me to build up and encourage other Christians by speaking to them of spiritual things.

- God has used me to proclaim timely and urgent messages or to give directions that have come to me through his Word and/or Spirit.

If this is a waiting gift for me,

- I receive spiritual insights from the Word and/or Spirit concerning people and issues, and I desire to express those insights.

- I am strongly motivated to declare the truth as God has revealed it to me.

- I am convinced that God wants me to speak out for him on social and moral issues of the day.

Ways to Use the Gift of Prophecy

Personal/informal uses:

- underscore the truth of God's Word to a friend

- lead my family to an awareness of God's answers to life's problems

- give guidance received from the Holy Spirit to other believers

Ministries within the church:

- preach a scripturally based message with compelling application to contemporary needs

- instruct a class studying current social problems

- speak a message from God to believers in a small group

- give directions that affect a congregation's future

Community-oriented ministries for Christ:

- speak out publicly on crucial moral or social issues
- write about political and social issues from a biblical perspective

Potential Liabilities in the Gift of Prophecy

Persons with this gift can sometimes tend to

- take personal pride in their ability to speak and persuade people.
- deviate from or go beyond the Scriptures (1 Corinthians 14:37-38).
- be so negative as to be a prophet of doom rather than a bearer of good news.
- be so blunt that people are put off by their manner.

Prophecy as a Responsibility of All Christians

In a sense, all Christians are prophets. Prophecy envisions a "forthtelling" of God's truth so that others may be touched by it. All Christians are responsible to speak forth the truth of God even if they may not have a gift to do it with extraordinary ability. Moses expressed a desire in line with this, saying, "I wish that all the LORD's people were prophets and that the LORD would put his Spirit on them!" (Numbers 11:29). The prophet Joel predicted that God would pour out his Spirit upon all flesh and that the "sons and daughters" of God's people would prophesy (Joel 2:28-29), and this word from the Lord was fulfilled on Pentecost day (Acts 2:16-17). Paul counseled believers to aim for a broad use of prophecy: "I would rather have [every one of] you prophesy" (1 Corinthians 14:5), and he even envisioned a worship service in which "everybody [was] prophesying" (14:24).

Discerning the Gift of Prophecy

1. What inclinations, insights, sensitivities, or concerns have I had that indicate I have the gift of prophecy?

2. How has God used this gift through me to affect the lives of other people?

3. Have others said things about me that have helped to confirm that I have this gift? If so, what?

4. In what ways could this gift be further used . . .

   a. in my personal relationships with friends, at home, or at work?

   b. in the church?

   c. in community-oriented ministries for Christ?

5. What problems or pitfalls, if any, have I encountered in using this gift?

Exploring Prophecy from Scripture

1. Read 1 Corinthians 14:1-25, 36-40. Summarize the main teaching of the Bible on prophecy as it appears in these verses.

2. How was prophecy used in Acts 15:32?

3. What happened through prophecy as reported in Acts 13:1-3?

4. What purpose was served by the prophecies of Agabus recorded in Acts 11:27-30 and Acts 21:10-14?

5. How should prophets conduct themselves in public worship, according to 1 Corinthians 14:29-33?

6. How should prophecy be received, according to 1 Thessalonians 5:20? How does this word about prophecy compare with Matthew 7:15-16? 1 Corinthians 14:29? 1 John 4:1-3?

7. According to Deuteronomy 18:20-22, what controls were placed on prophets? How was it possible to detect a false prophet?

SERVICE

Definition

The special Spirit-given ability to see and meet the needs of others by willingly helping them in practical ways.

Service as a Spiritual Gift

Wherever we look in the home, the church, or the community, we see hundreds of things that need tending to. Many of these things require no more than the ability to identify a task and the willingness to get it done. That's essentially what the gift of service is about—seeing and meeting needs. The needs or tasks may be menial or unattractive to others, but they are willingly assumed by the person with the gift of service. The Greek word for "service," *diakonia*, has its roots in a word meaning "to run errands."

Sometimes when the New Testament uses the word *diakonia*, it refers to waiting on tables (Luke 10:40); sometimes it relates to works of charity (Acts 6:1); and sometimes to the ministry of the Word (Acts 6:4). But as a spiritual gift, *diakonia* (service) is shown most clearly in those who make themselves available to reach out to a personal or material need. Jesus modeled this gift best by coming "not . . . to be served but to serve" (Mark 10:45). Phoebe, "a servant of the church in Cenchrea," exhibited the gift of service by being "a great help to many people" (Romans 16:1-2). Titus demonstrated the gift of service by carrying money gifts collected for the needy in Jerusalem (2 Corinthians 8:16-19).

Elsewhere in Scripture the gift of service is described as the gift of helping others (1 Corinthians 12:28). The idea in helping others is basically the same as service. Helping involves taking a burden on yourself instead of leaving it on someone else.

The gift of service must not be regarded as unimportant because it doesn't involve prestigious skills like the kind required for preaching or leadership. It's a valuable gift sorely needed in the church.

Characteristics of the Person with the Gift of Service

If this is a working gift for me,

- I enjoy doing tasks that help others minister effectively.
- I am not put off by menial tasks but do them willingly as long as they help to build the body of Christ.
- I find practical ways of helping others, and I gain satisfaction from doing this.

If this is a waiting gift for me,

- I sense when others need a helping hand, and I am ready to give it.
- I love to serve, and I often take the initiative to meet needs.
- I am able to identify needs quickly, and I can be counted on for almost any kind of help.

Ways to Use the Gift of Service

Personal/informal uses:

- be a "good Samaritan"
- help a busy single parent with children
- assist a widow or elderly person with a difficult home-maintenance task

Ministries within the church:

- help out in the nursery
- do kitchen work for church functions
- be involved in a refugee-resettlement program
- help meet the needs of members who are sick, disadvantaged, or poor

Community-oriented ministries for Christ:

- take part in a community clean-up effort
- remodel homes for disadvantaged families
- work in a used-clothing center

Potential Liabilities in the Gift of Service

Persons with the spiritual gift of service can sometimes tend to

- find more self-esteem in doing than in being.
- become worried and upset about many things and miss the "one thing needed" (Luke 10:41-42).
- never say no, get over-involved, and then feel they are being abused.
- use their gift to secure the affection of others.
- neglect home and family while serving others.

Service as a Responsibility of All Christians

All Christians are responsible to serve. They are challenged to be "the servant of all" (Mark 9:35) and to live like their Lord, who came "not . . . to be served, but to serve" (Matthew 20:28). All believers have a duty to "help the weak" (1 Thessalonians 5:14), says Paul, and to "serve one another in love. [For] the entire law is summed up in a single command: 'Love your neighbor as yourself'" (Galatians 5:13-14).

Discerning the Gift of Service

1. What inner inclinations, insights, sensitivities, or concerns have I had that indicate I have the gift of service?

2. How has God used this gift through me to affect the lives of other people?

3. Have others said things about me that have helped to confirm that I have this gift? If so, what?

4. In what ways could this gift be further used ...

   a. in my personal relationships at home, with friends, or at work?

   b. in the church?

   c. in community-oriented ministries for Christ?

5. What problems or pitfalls, if any, have I encountered in using this gift?

Exploring Service from Scripture

1. Read Romans 12:7. Write out the part of the verse that identifies the gift of service.

2. What liability in the gift of service do we learn from the story of Mary and Martha in Luke 10:38-42?

3. How did Phoebe's life and ministry, as recorded in Romans 16:1-2, illustrate the gift of service?

4. Read 2 Timothy 1:16-18. What can we learn from the example of Onesiphorus about the gift of service and how he helped Paul?

5. With what attitude did Stephanas and his household serve the church, according to 1 Corinthians 16:15-18? What difference did their ministry make in the church?

SHEPHERDING

Definition

The special Spirit-given ability to keep watch over, care for, and feed members of the body of Christ, guiding, admonishing, and discipling them toward spiritual maturity.

Shepherding as a Spiritual Gift

Shepherding is included as a gift because the Greek word for "pastor" or "shepherd" is found in Ephesians 4:11 among the list of gifted persons serving the church. Often this gift is called pastoring. We use the word "shepherd" here to avoid confusing the gift with the position of the professional pastor. A person does not need to be an ordained pastor or to be theologically trained in order to have this gift.

A person who has the gift of shepherding may hold the formal position of elder or overseer (bishop). The words for "shepherd," "elder," and "overseer" ("bishop") seem to be interchangeable in Scripture. Most likely they give us three different views of a single ministry. The word "shepherd" speaks of the person who ministers pastorally. The word "elder" points to one's honored place in the Christian community. And the word "overseer" tells us how the work gets done.

The person who has the gift of shepherding watches over, cares for, feeds (John 21:17; Acts 20:28a; 1 Peter 5:2), guides (Isaiah 40:11; John 21:16), and protects (Acts 20:28b-29) other believers. The shepherd will ordinarily be "able to teach" (1 Timothy 3:2; Ephesians 4:11) and will be able to "encourage others by sound doctrine and refute those who oppose it" (Titus 1:9). A shepherd is also called to equip and enable others so that they may be built up and grow into Christlike maturity (Ephesians 4:12-13). Persons gifted as shepherds do their work willingly and eagerly, operating not with heavy-handed authority but by means of a good example (1 Peter 5:1-3).

Characteristics of the Spiritually Gifted Shepherd

If this is a working gift for me,

- I have assumed responsibility for the spiritual well-being of others who have grown spiritually through my assistance, guided by the Holy Spirit.

- I am enabled by the Spirit to provide ongoing care, spiritual nourishment, and protection to other believers.

- the Lord has used me to watch over and guide other Christians and nurture them toward spiritual maturity.

If this is a waiting gift for me,

- I am concerned that the spiritual needs of believers must be met and am willing to be personally involved in nurturing and discipling ministries.

- I sense in myself a shepherd's instinct when I know of Christians who need spiritual counsel.

- I like being with other Christians and am willing to be involved if they are in need of counsel or guidance.

Ways to Use the Gift of Shepherding

Personal/informal uses:

- disciple a new convert

- guide a roommate toward spiritual growth

- disciple family members

Ministries within the church:

- become a youth group counselor

- serve as an elder

- lead a discipling class

- lead a small group

Community-oriented ministries for Christ:

- conduct a prison ministry

- do volunteer work for a child-guidance clinic

- lead campus Bible studies or spiritual-growth groups

Potential Liabilities in the Gift of Shepherding

Persons with the gift of shepherding can sometimes tend to

- have difficulty saying "no" to additional involvement in ministering pastorally.

- be so sensitive that they will not confront those who need admonition.

- allow those to whom they minister to become overly dependent.

Shepherding as a Responsibility of All Christians

A shepherd is one who tends a flock by feeding, guiding, leading, and watching over the sheep. There is a sense in which every Christian is called to be a shepherd. All are to care for one another (1 Corinthians 12:25), guide one another (Proverbs 11:14; 15:22), and seek the welfare of one another (Romans 15:2), as a shepherd does for his sheep. The lambs of the flock require special concern (Matthew

10:42). Parents are shepherds to their children. Teachers of children shepherd their lambs with loving care. Youth counselors, coaches, and high school vocational counselors shepherd their charges through many situations. Not all of the persons in these positions have the gift of shepherding. Many are simply exercising a responsibility out of a heart of love.

Discerning the Gift of Shepherding

1. What inclinations, insights, sensitivities, or concerns have I had that indicate I have the gift of shepherding?

2. How has God used this gift through me to affect the lives of other people?

3. Have others said things about me that have helped to confirm that I have this gift? If so, what?

4. In what ways could this gift be further used . . .

   a. in my personal relationships at home, with friends, or at work?

   b. in the church?

   c. in community-oriented ministries for Christ?

5. What problems or pitfalls, if any, have I encountered in using this gift?

Exploring Shepherding from Scripture

1. What is the task of the shepherd/pastor as described in Ephesians 4:11-13?

2. What are the significant things we learn about a shepherd's role from the words and examples of Jesus in John 10:1-18?

3. What do we learn about the shepherd's task from Ezekiel 34:1-6, 15? What will happen if the shepherd fails?

4. In 1 Peter 5:1-4 the shepherd is an elder of the church. What must he do? How must he do it? What is his reward?

SPEAKING IN TONGUES

Definition

The special Spirit-given ability to speak in sounds and utterances previously unknown to the speaker.

Speaking in Tongues as a Spiritual Gift

The gift of speaking in tongues is clearly reported in Scripture. It was given to the company of 120 believers on Pentecost day (Acts 1:15; 2:4), to the family of Cornelius after they responded to Peter's preaching (Acts 10:46), and to a group of Ephesian believers (Acts 19:6). The apostle Paul also spoke in tongues and expressed his desire that other Christians would also be able to do so (1 Corinthians 14:5, 18). In some cases the tongue that is spoken is language that is understood by someone else present, as at Pentecost. In other cases the tongue-speaking may be direct communication with God (1 Corinthians 14:2; see also 13:1).

In the biblical reports, tongues were used in two different ways. In 1 Corinthians 14:2 we read that tongues is a form of prayer or praise language to God. The believer uses tongues in personal devotions as a form of intimate, direct communication with God that transcends human interpersonal communication. It has the effect of deepening and enriching one's prayer life, building up one's faith, and liberating the Spirit within. Although the person speaking in tongues does not understand the message, God receives it and is blessed by it. This use of tongues may also take the form of spiritual song (1 Corinthians 14:14-15; Ephesians 5:19). Paul desires that "all would speak in tongues," suggesting that it is a desirable gift for every believer.

Speaking in tongues is also a "sign gift." In 1 Corinthians 14:22 Paul specifically notes that this gift is a "sign . . . for unbelievers" when tongues are used in worship (see also Mark 16:17). The tongues spoken at Pentecost demonstrated the effect of this sign. Startled and amazed by what they heard the apostles speaking, the crowd asked, "What does this mean?" (Acts 2:12). Then Peter spoke God's word to the crowd (prophecy), and as a result many people were converted and brought into the church that day (Acts 2:14-41). In such a context, speaking in tongues serves as a sign of the presence and power of God and grabs the attention of those present so that they can hear God's word and come to repentance (see 1 Corinthians 14:23-25).

While the gift of speaking in tongues is valuable, it is also potentially problematic. Paul warns that tongue-speaking can be disruptive and divisive. Without love the gift is useless (1 Corinthians 13:1). In public worship the use of tongues should be limited, and interpretation should be available (14:27). If there is no one to interpret, the tongues should not be spoken for others to hear (14:28). Believers who speak in tongues should pray for the gift of interpretation (14:13). In public worship, prophecy is recommended over tongues for its value in bringing understanding (14:18-19, 24). Balance is important. Believers who pray in tongues should pray with the mind also (14:15-19).

Here are some cautions to keep in mind. First of all, the gift of speaking in tongues is not usually associated with extreme emotion or ecstasy. The speaker remains in control and can choose when and where to exercise the gift. Further, although tongues often accompanies a personal experience of empowerment by the Holy Spirit, it is not to be considered the initial evidence of being filled with the Holy Spirit. Neither is it a special mark of spiritual maturity. Finally, to avoid over-emphasizing the gift and its value, remember that speaking in tongues was never a major emphasis of Jesus or his disciples. The Bible has no reference to Jesus speaking in tongues.

Characteristics of the Person with the Gift of Tongues

If this is a working gift for me,

- I regularly pray in an unknown language.
- I am being built up in the faith by my use of this gift.
- sometimes I am so caught up in wonder and love for God that I pray in the Spirit.

If this is a waiting gift for me,

- I delight in opening up my deepest self to the supernatural influence of the Holy Spirit and letting him take over my tongue.
- I sometimes feel a flow of life and love within me that transcends the rational.
- in expressing praise to God, I frequently come to the point where cognitive speech no longer conveys the meaning.

Ways to Use the Gift of Speaking in Tongues

Personal/informal use:

- in personal devotions
- quietly when in public worship
- as a trigger to release and nurture other gifts

Ministries within the church:

- in public worship when an interpreter is present
- in a small group when praying for needs I don't understand very well

- in a midweek church prayer meeting

Community-oriented ministries for Christ:

- as a "sign" in an evangelistic service
- praying for neighbors in a neighborhood prayer ministry

Potential Liabilities in the Gift of Speaking in Tongues

The person with this gift can sometimes tend to

- exercise the gift without love.
- make speaking in tongues the norm for spiritual maturity.
- use the gift for self-glory.

Speaking in Tongues as a Responsibility of All Christians

Many Christians who are both mature and effective in ministry have never spoken in tongues. That's okay. In 1 Corinthians 12:30 Paul's question "Do all speak in tongues?" assumes a negative answer. However, underlying the practical expressions of this gift are spiritual values that are the responsibility of all believers, such as praising God in prayer, yielding control of our tongues to the Holy Spirit, and speaking for Christ in ways that gain the attention of unbelievers.

Discerning the Gift of Speaking in Tongues

1. What inclinations, insights, sensitivities, or concerns have I had that indicate I have the gift of speaking in tongues?

2. How has God used this gift through me to affect the lives of other people?

3. Have others said things about me that have helped to confirm that I have this gift? If so, what?

4. In what ways could this gift be further used . . .

   a. in my personal relationships at home, with friends, or at work?

   b. in the church?

   c. in community-oriented ministries for Christ?

5. What problems or pitfalls, if any, have I encountered in using this gift?

Exploring the Gift of Speaking in Tongues from Scripture

1. Write out the phrases from 1 Corinthians 12:10, 28-29 that refer to the gift of speaking in tongues.

2. Acts 2:1-4, 38; 10:44-47, and 19:1-6 describe Spirit outpourings on groups of early believers that resulted in speaking in tongues. What do these events have in common? In what ways do they differ?

3. Read the following passages. Why has God given tongues to the church?

• 1 Corinthians 14:2

• 1 Corinthians 14:4

• 1 Corinthians 14:22

•1 Corinthians 14:26

4. What cautions and controls does Paul recommend in the following passages about speaking in tongues?

• 1 Corinthians 13:1

• 1 Corinthians 14:13

• 1 Corinthians 14:15-17

• 1 Corinthians 14:27-28

5. How does speaking in tongues compare in value to prophecy, according to 1 Corinthians 14:1-6, 18-19, 22?

TEACHING

Definition

The special Spirit-given ability to clearly and effectively communicate biblical truths and information that helps believers mature in the faith, building up the body of Christ.

Teaching as a Spiritual Gift

The gift of teaching is listed in all three of the main gift passages in the New Testament. Each of the passages teaches something different about the gift. According to 1 Corinthians 12:28, the gift of teaching ranks high, being associated with the gifts of apostleship and prophecy. In Ephesians 4:11-12, where it is closely associated with shepherding (pastoring), it is given to the church "to prepare God's people for works of service, so that the body of Christ may be built up." In Romans 12:7 the emphasis is upon using the gift for the advantage of the church.

Jesus clearly exercised this gift. Matthew reports that "when he saw the crowds, he went up on a mountainside . . . and began to teach them" (Matthew 5:1-2). What he taught them is known today as the Sermon on the Mount. Jesus' teaching was clear and effective. He used the stuff of everyday life to illustrate difficult teachings about the kingdom: sheep, wine, water, candles, leaven, and so on. His parables attracted and held the attention of his audiences. After Jesus ascended to heaven, the Holy Spirit took up a teaching ministry, just as the Lord had promised: "The Counselor, the Holy Spirit, whom the Father will send in my name, will teach you all things" (John 14:26).

The apostles whom Jesus had chosen to carry on his work and to lay the foundation of the church also exercised the gift. "They never stopped teaching and proclaiming the good news that Jesus is the Christ" (Acts 5:42). The apostle Paul, while under house arrest in Rome for the sake of Christ and the gospel, "welcomed all who came to see him . . . preached the kingdom of God, and taught about the Lord Jesus Christ" (Acts 28:30-31). The great objective for which he labored, "struggling with all [Christ's] energy," was to "proclaim [Christ], admonishing and teaching everyone with all wisdom" (Colossians 1:28-29). Apollos also excelled in teaching. "He was a learned man," says Acts 18:24-25, "with a thorough knowledge of the Scriptures. . . . He spoke with great fervor and taught about Jesus accurately" (Acts 18:24-25).

The Bible gives a few cautions about teachers and teaching. Believers are warned, "Not many of you should presume to be teachers . . . because you know that we who teach will be judged more strictly" (James 3:1). Peter cautions, "There will be false teachers among you. . . . They will secretly introduce destructive heresies, even denying the sovereign Lord. . . . Many will follow their shameful ways and will bring the way of truth into disrepute" (2 Peter 2:1-2).

Teaching was obviously important to the New Testament church. Most of what was written in the gospels and epistles came from those who were exercising this gift. Again and again, the gift of teaching preceded the New Testament's urgent appeals to practical Christian living. Teaching remains an important gift in the Christian community today.

Characteristics of the Spiritually Gifted Teacher

If this is a working gift for me,

- lights of understanding go on as I explain the Bible or some aspect of the Christian life in an instructional setting, guided by the Holy Spirit.

- I am able to communicate truth clearly and effectively in such a way that others learn.

- I usually can sense what it takes to hold the interest of those I teach.

If this is a waiting gift for me,

- I have a strong desire to communicate truths and/or information that will help believers mature in the faith and build up the church.

- I am motivated to get involved when there is an obvious need for knowledge or insight.

- I get excited about discovering new ideas I can share with others.

Ways to Use the Gift of Teaching

Personal/informal uses:

- teach my own children Bible truths

- lead a friend in a one-to-one Bible study

- clarify religious issues for an acquaintance

Ministries within the church:

- serve as a church school teacher

- lead an adult Bible study

- lead the lesson in a small group

Community-oriented ministries for Christ:

- teach school

- instruct in a life-enrichment class

Potential Liabilities in the Gift of Teaching

A spiritually gifted teacher can sometimes tend to

- be more concerned with head knowledge than with heart knowledge.

- communicate too much information too quickly.

- be more content-oriented than person-oriented.

- assume that those being instructed have a high interest in the subject.

Teaching as a Responsibility of All Christians

To teach is to impart knowledge to others. All Christians, whether by actions or words, do this. "By this time you ought to be teachers," says the writer to the Hebrews, admonishing immature Christians (Hebrews 5:12). And Paul speaks to all Christians when he says, "Let the word of Christ dwell in you richly as you teach and admonish one another with all wisdom" (Colossians 3:16). The whole church is given a teaching role in the Great Commission's challenge to teach disciples "to obey everything" Jesus has commanded (Matthew 28:20). When it comes to content, the Bible is our fundamental source for "teaching . . . and training in righteousness" (2 Timothy 3:16). "Everything that was written in the past was written to teach us," says Paul, "so that through endurance and the encouragement of the Scriptures we might have hope" (Romans 15:4).

Discerning the Gift of Teaching

1. What inclinations, insights, sensitivities, or concerns have I had that indicate I have the gift of teaching?

2. How has God used this gift through me to affect the lives of other people?

3. Have others said things about me that have helped to confirm that I have this gift? Is so, what?

4. In what ways could this gift be further used . . .

   a. in my personal relationships with friends, at home, or at work?

   b. in the church?

   c. in community-oriented ministries for Christ?

5. What problems or pitfalls, if any, have I encountered in using this gift?

Exploring Teaching from Scripture

1. Write out the phrases from Romans 12:7, 1 Corinthians 12:28, and Ephesians 4:11 that identify the gift of teaching.

2. Read Acts 18:24-28. What can we see in Apollos's example that tells us about the gift of teaching?

3. What can keep the gifted teacher from pride? (See 1 Corinthians 3:5-9; 4:6.)

4. Read Acts 20:18-21, 27; 28:30-31. What can we see in Paul's example that tells us about the gift of teaching?

5. What is the goal of teaching, according to Ephesians 4:13-14?

WISDOM

Definition

The special Spirit-given ability to see situations and issues from God's perspective and to apply God-given insights to specific areas of need.

Wisdom as a Spiritual Gift

The spiritual gift of wisdom mentioned in 1 Corinthians 12:8 is the ability to apply knowledge in a fitting way. It is that supernatural insight which shows the way through. The person with this gift often turns the key that unlocks a difficult problem, offers pertinent spiritual counsel, knows how to handle a difficult person, or brings about a reconciliation between alienated persons.

Jesus possessed and exercised this gift. People were impressed by the wisdom with which he spoke (Mark 6:2). His perspective was clearly given him by the Father in heaven (Matthew 11:25-27). His words of wisdom shone through in the perceptive answers he gave to those who tried to trap him (Matthew 21:23-27; 22:23-33; Luke 20:20-26). We see his wisdom most clearly in the cross (1 Corinthians 1:18-25). No wonder Paul said that in him "are hidden all the treasures of wisdom and knowledge" (Colossians 2:3).

The disciples were promised special wisdom in moments of special challenge (Luke 21:14-15), and they gave evidence of possessing this gift in the situations Jesus described (Acts 3:11-4:20). The apostle Paul also wrote his letters with God-given wisdom (2 Peter 3:15-16).

The source of all wisdom is God himself, as Scripture reminds us in Proverbs 2:6, "The Lord gives wisdom," and in 1 Corinthians 2:13, "We speak, not in words taught us by human wisdom but in words taught by the Spirit." Divine wisdom is contrasted with worldly wisdom, which is "foolishness in God's sight" (1 Corinthians 3:19).

Characteristics of the Person with the Gift of Wisdom

If this is a working gift for me,

- I often give practical insights to people which help to solve problems.
- God gives me insights in situations in which I have had no previous knowledge.
- I am able to apply spiritual knowledge in practical ways.

If this is a waiting gift for me,

- I sometimes have extraordinary, God-given insights into situations, but I am not given to express these insights.

- I have a great interest in seeing spiritual knowledge applied in real-life situations.
- I often know what to do, how to do it, and when to do it in situations that leave others puzzled.

Ways to Use the Gift of Wisdom

Personal/informal uses:

- counsel friends who bring their problems to me
- apply scriptural principles to my own life
- live out the truth of James 3:17 ("The wisdom that comes from heaven is first of all pure; then peace-loving, considerate, submissive, full of mercy and good fruit, impartial and sincere.")

Ministries within the church:

- serve as a member of a counseling team
- help guide the congregation through a troublesome time
- be available to members of the church who may be facing financial difficulties, family problems, business reversals, and so on

Community-oriented ministries for Christ:

- serve in a governmental or judicial position or as a counselor to such officials
- serve as an arbitrator or negotiator between sparring parties or groups
- serve on a jury

Potential Liabilities in the Gift of Wisdom

A person with this gift can sometimes tend to

- become overly self-confident and begin to offer human wisdom rather than heavenly wisdom.
- think of himself more highly than he should.
- become impatient with those who do not listen to what she has to say.

Wisdom as a Responsibility of All Christians

All Christians are called to get wisdom (Proverbs 4:7). The person who finds it is blessed (Proverbs 3:13-14). God offers wisdom to all who please him (Ecclesiastes 2:26). James declares that wisdom is available to all who need it and ask for it in faith (James 1:5-6). Jesus promises wisdom to all who are tested (Luke 21:15). The wisest thing a Christian can do is to hear the words of Christ and live by them (Matthew 7:24).

Discerning the Gift of Wisdom

1. What inclinations, insights, sensitivities, or concerns have I had that indicate I have the gift of wisdom?

2. How has God used this gift through me to affect the lives of other people?

3. Have others said things about me that have helped to confirm that I have this gift? If so, what?

4. In what ways could this gift be further used . . .

   a. in my personal relationships at home, with friends, or at work?

   b. in the church?

   c. in community-oriented ministries for Christ?

5. What problems or pitfalls, if any, have I encountered in using this gift?

Exploring Wisdom from Scripture

1. Write out the phrase from 1 Corinthians 12:8 that confirms wisdom as a spiritual gift.

2. What can we learn from Matthew 21:23-27 about Jesus' use of this gift? From Luke 20:20-26?

3. What do you see in Acts 4:8-13, 18-20 to indicate that Peter and John had the gift of wisdom? (See also Luke 21:15.)

4. What is one purpose of the message of wisdom, according to Colossians 1:28?

5. Read James 3:13-17. What distinguishes the truly wise person from a worldly-wise person?